CASTLES & RUINS

CASTLES & RUINS

UNRAVELING FAMILY MYSTERIES &
LITERARY LEGACY IN THE IRISH COUNTRYSIDE

RUE MATTHIESSEN

Cover design by Blair Seagram and Kevin Breen
Book design by Kevin Breen

ISBN: 978-1-957607-25-2
Cataloging-in-Publication Data is available upon request

Manufactured in the United States of America

Published by Latah Books
www.latahbooks.com

This book is dedicated to the strong and generous women who each in their own way saw the empty spaces that were left, and helped me to drag a self out of the ashes. I am forever indebted and grateful to them.

In order of appearance:
Dorothy Sherry, Maria Matthiessen, and Merete Galesi

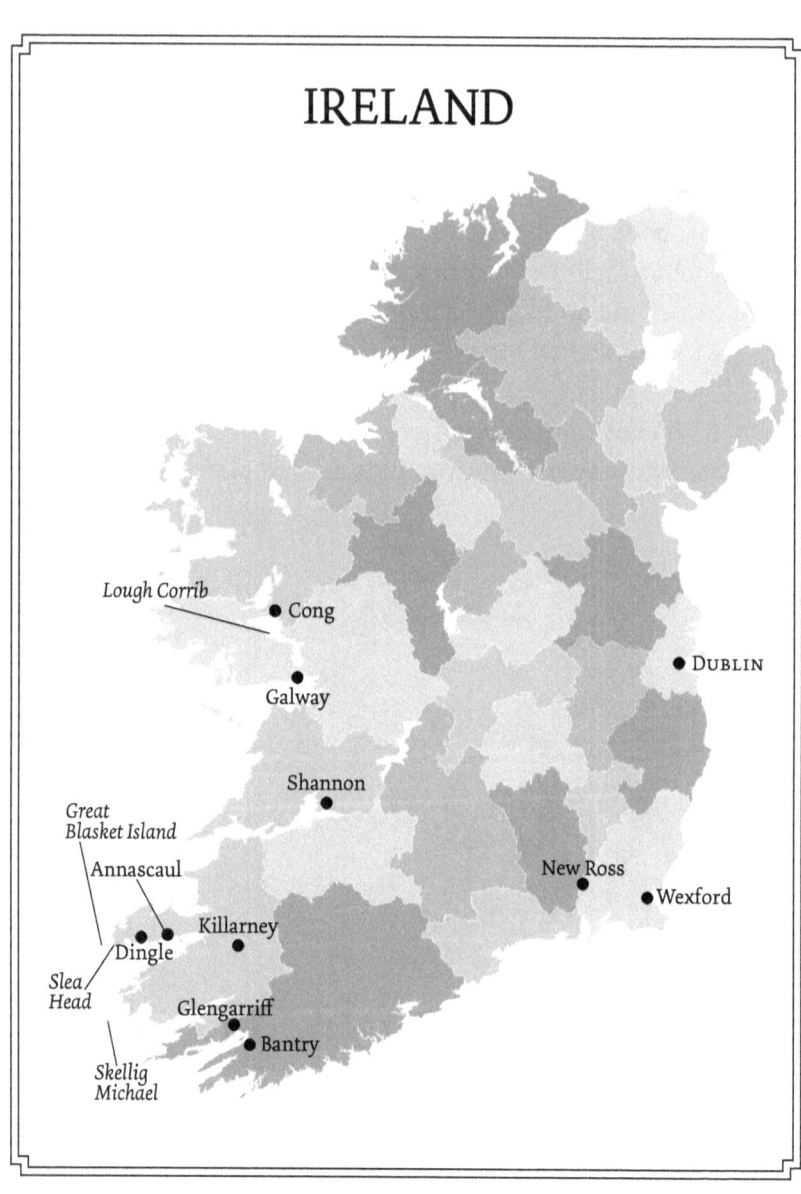

IRELAND

Lough Corrib

● Cong

● DUBLIN

● Galway

● Shannon

Great
Blasket Island

Annascaul

New Ross ●

● Wexford

Killarney

Dingle

●

Slea
Head

Glengarriff

● Bantry

Skellig
Michael

Contents

Prologue: Annaghkeen   1

1. Smash the Pane   9

2. Real Life   23

3. Tinkers   37

4. The Ancients   49

5. Fallen Gods   59

6. Ghost House Walk   83

7. LSD and Zen   103

8. The Girl in the Raincoat   125

9. Hell's Bells   145

10. Hoko Debby   167

11. Old Timers   191

12. The Storybook   215

Prologue: Annaghkeen

At the age of seven in the summer of 1965, I lived on an island in Galway, Ireland with my mother Deborah Love, father Peter Matthiessen, and my twelve-year-old stepbrother Luke from my father's first marriage. The rare opportunity to rent such a place came to us through my father's profession as a writer, and by extension his circle of artistic and literary friends. Writer Don Braider and his wife Carol were friends of my father's first wife Patsy Southgate, daughter of Richard Southgate, Chief of Protocol for the Roosevelt White House. The Braiders had lived in Ireland for two years and had enthusiastically connected him with the O'Connells, owners of the island and house.

Across the waterway from our island in Ireland that summer was Annaghkeen Castle, erected by the de Burgh family in the 1300s. For our purposes, it lent a magical air to all that it surveyed, including our island with its own pine wood, a monkey puzzle tree, and an ancient cairn. A retaining wall ringed the side facing the castle. From the edge of it, the lake waters were gray-brown and spooky, even on sunny days. The water in Lough Corrib was good enough to drink, and we did. My brother and I swam every day, diving from the dock or the retaining wall.

That summer and always, aside from his travels for research, my father never had to be any particular place to do his job. It was easy to pack up for a month, for three months, for six months, sometimes with family in tow but more often on his own, to gather research and write. To some, this might seem a great freedom, and in many ways it was. But one idiosyncrasy of not having to be tied to anyplace can also extend to *anyone*, and that became pervasive throughout the culture of our family in its various forms over the following years. Through a myriad of manifestations, my father always had a stunning ability to move on, sometimes shucking earlier associations like fresh snow from his shoulders.

My first taste of this shapeshifting, always-forward flow, this ability to land somewhere and re-create ourselves, or at least try to, came that summer of 1965. As I was only seven, I couldn't have known that there was another aspect of the trip—my parents had planned it as an effort to save their marriage. The tense atmosphere between them was a constant weather pattern, each season recognizable—gathering storm clouds a cue to ramp up defenses, and the good parts very good, more so for their impermanence—while signaling another cue to let some air from the balloon and fly a little closer to earth for fear of crashing.

At home in New York, my father's earlier books, written in the mid-to-late-fifties, weren't big sellers. But in the summer of 1965, *At Play in the Fields of the Lord* was going to press, and it would be his breakout book. There were parties with stars of the art and literary world dropping by our remodeled home regularly—writer and bon vivant George Plimpton and his wife Freddie, writer William Styron and his wife Rose, writer John P. Marquand Jr., and Joe Fox, my father's editor at Random House, to name a few.

From a young age, it was impossible for me to miss that there was something different about my father. He drew people to him, whether he wanted them around or not. He often wanted to be alone, working. Yet somehow his considerable self-containment leant him tremendous personal power. He was absolutely a star. He was charismatic, he was glamorous, and so was the world that he lived in. He had a gaze that was memorable, and sometimes frightening. It bore right through you. Was it depth of vision? All seeing? Was it wisdom? Was it something bottomless in him? Some great void?

As my father's career took hold, he needed the household to run well; he might've been surprised to discover that his intellectual and ambitious second wife was not domestic in any way. Instead, my mother wanted to practice Japanese tea ceremony in a special room she had made up with rice-paper screens and tatami mats, or walk on the beach at the foot of our road, or sit at her own desk writing down all that she thought and wondered about. It was a good thing she did not defer her hopes. The journal she kept in Ireland would become her first and last book. It was called *Annaghkeen*, after the castle. Over the course of my life, I would read it many, many times.

In their early years, it was she who went first to Alan Watts lectures, did yoga, and practiced Zen. I remember her getting out her yoga book (with photographs of an emaciated swami in what looked like a diaper) and practicing yoga on the bathroom floor. Her friends thought she'd gone mad. She didn't care. When we traveled to Italy in 1968 and lived in a castle with expat friends from New York, my parents and their friends took a pure LSD that came in blue liquid form because LSD was purported to be like "twenty years of psychoanalysis in a vial."

By that time, partly due to my father's constant affairs, their marriage was in deep trouble. My mother treated the evidence of his dalliances in the same radical spirit—she dropped me off at a babysitter and went to the city to meet up with her admirers. There were many to choose from. LSD became another drastic remedy, pushed to the limit in sessions in New York City and Italy. She would pile on the dosage if she thought there was anything she might learn about how to fix herself, her husband, or her third marriage.

For me, as a child at Annaghkeen, the mood in our little house on the island was still insulated from all of that, if only by virtue of the earliness of things, and me being very young, and the many miles between us and home in New York. Even if I had been able to see into the future, I could not have understood the enormity of the changes that were there, just waiting for us to step into them.

On the island, my father strained toward his work, usually tucked away somewhere outside where he wouldn't be bothered—a yellow legal pad balanced on his knee, and bird and wildlife reference guides in a neat pile beside him. Meanwhile, my mother was most content while reading Yeats and difficult fiction like *Finnegans Wake* and thinking about big questions, often staring off across the water. Sometimes, we'd sneak off together to Ross Errilly, a nearby ruin of a Franciscan convent and church. There, while picking around worn stones with her walking stick, she heard whispered answers of a sort that she wrote about in *Annaghkeen*.

Other days, my father and Luke would get the motorboat going and take us fishing or to the Ower House hotel a few miles down the shore for dinner. We went to Inchagoill Island to see the Lugnaedon Stone, which had an early Christian cross. We visited Cong Abbey, eight hundred years old, and Inishmaine Abbey in County Mayo from about the same period. Having abandoned the Episcopal Church of their youths, my mother and father were still deeply contemplative by nature. So we went to these ancient abbeys, churches, and monasteries again and again. I felt their wistfulness in these places. There was a sense of being almost finished, of coming apart from each other and from us, and coming back together, possibly, at some future point. What this point was—where it was—I had no idea.

Ireland was their attempt to stop time. Perhaps in the silence, the reasoning that drew my parents to a life of letters— and each other—would find new vigor. Away from the whirl and the demands of running a big house, my mother would have a chance to study and write and find her own voice, my father to fish and fossil hunt, bird watch, and unwind. Galway was ancient and fascinatingly undisturbed, yet neither of them could have been prepared for what they found or did not find when all the distractions were removed.

Upon our return to the States in the fall of 1965, my mother went to work on developing her journals, and mine, into *Annaghkeen*. When her book first came out, I was eleven. I remember the stacks of signed copies on the living room table, waiting to be given out to family and friends. The dust jacket was her black and white photo of the castle under a tall, cloud-pocked sky. The picture wrapped around to the back to show the bungalow and a flurry of pines looking on. For me, the philosophical parts were too dense, so I skipped them. I concentrated instead on the parts that I had written, that were taken from a journal she'd encouraged me to keep that summer. Reading my own seven-year-old ruminations about fairies and my pet snail "Wilbert," complete with misspelled words, was thrilling. I wasn't interested in the rest. When I was older and she was gone, I'd read the book again, devouring paragraphs, looking for clues in what she had said or done that might be illuminating. My own memory became garlanded with hers, creating more of a mystery about what that time had been.

After Ireland, she and my father hung on, the drama subsiding for brief sunny periods or whenever they had a stretch of time apart. *At Play in the Fields of the Lord* was published, and the movie rights were sold. He bought an otter-skin coat for her and a gray wool coat with a nutria collar for himself. They jokingly called these the "success coats." In 1967, he published *The Shorebirds of North America*, and in 1969, *Sal Si Puedes*.

In April 1970, *Annaghkeeen* was published. About five months later, my mother was diagnosed with ovarian cancer. I was grateful to have *Annaghkeen*. People often said what a lucky thing it was to have a book that could be a touchstone throughout the years, like having a visit with her. By the time I was married, years had gone by without reading it. I had been too busy.

Paradoxically, the memory of my mother became more vivid as my son Emmett grew older, especially as he approached the age I was during our *Annaghkeen* summer. Echoes of her, which had always been present, grew louder. The worn copy of *Annaghkeen* in the bookcase spoke to me every time my eye rested on it. I began to wonder about Annaghkeen Castle, the actual *place*. Having survived at least a millennium, surely it must still be there. In all those years in between, I hadn't been back to Ireland, not even to bounce through on the way to somewhere else. So I began to think about going back and seeing if I could find it again. I talked to my husband Steve. Though his forebears were Irish, he had never been there, so he liked the idea. It looked as though we would have the time to go in the summer. We'd have to rent out our house near the sea on Long Island, and there would be a lot of work to do.

For awhile, at night after Emmett was in bed, I pored over maps and books about Ireland from the library and from Steve's dad's bookshelves. In those pages, I found many Irish antiquities but never a mention of Annaghkeen Castle. I had imprecise coordinates from my mother's book amounting to a few paragraphs, and that was all. It was exciting to look through all of this stuff and think about the trip. Unlike the few other trips we had taken—to the Caribbean or New Hampshire in the summer—it helped me to think of the whole thing as a treasure hunt in a country unfamiliar to Steve and unfamiliar to me since I was young. I was brimming with anticipation but also with an underlying sneaky feeling, like continuing to listen in on a phone line after the other person believes that you have hung up. Ireland was my parents' story, not mine. I was just a kid. What would I find? I was a little afraid and intensely curious at the same time.

We would travel hard, never staying anywhere for long. We'd include a few of the more famous destinations my mother had written about—Ross Errilly Friary and Cong—but also leave a certain amount up to chance because it would be more interesting that way. The treasure, I told myself, was to lay eyes again on the castle and the little house across the waterway where we had lived, and to think about those years and learn something about this place my parents had chosen for us that summer. Emmett could learn about the country of his forebears, and so could we. Keep it simple, I said, flicking through my pages of plans, having no idea what was to come.

Smash the Pane

While it was important to remove ourselves from the place we were, we could really be going anywhere. Yet Ireland drew us, for it is not yet of the world, but belongs still to the earth, far more ancient and primitive and passionate, and there men listen to the strange voices that they hear, and are respectful.

(Italicized excerpts, including this one, are from Deborah Love's *Annaghkeen*, except where otherwise noted.)

I told Steve that this was most likely the land of tea, not coffee. Steve, a person who needs strong coffee like a car needs gas, was pale. In the arrivals hall at Shannon, we found a Starbucks knockoff that looked good to me, though he shook his head. Steve has a canny sense about these things and often has hunches about restaurants that turn out to be true. It was our only choice, however. A woman at the counter with the alertness of a college professor took our order: a double espresso for Steve, a small coffee for me, and a hot chocolate for Emmett.

I was dazzled to be breathing Irish air again, and tired, as were we all. The woman served us, for the price of Starbucks, a weak brew not much better than instant. The coffee didn't matter, I will never forget her—the first Irish person I had spoken to in forty-one years. It was as if she knew the whole story. Or maybe, while working in an airport, with people tumbling off planes, she felt that in some way she might represent the entire nation. Her smooth face was kind and patient, and her green smock matched the hue of the big green sign above. She brought extra milk for Emmett's hot chocolate because it was too hot and was so polite and warm that tears came to my eyes. We sat in a circle around a plastic table, gathering up pieces of ourselves and looking around. Six-year-old Emmett drank sloppily, stunned by the experience of hurtling through the sky all night to alight four thousand miles away from home.

Ireland was, as advertised, a riot of greens. As we drove south toward the Dingle Peninsula, the fields were lumpy with grass so green it looked lit from within. There were smells of what I guessed to be peat fires, and cows, which I remembered. The fields stretched for miles left and right of the highway, divided by stone walls or dense bouquets of trees with a rustling softness, the sight of which was also intensely familiar. Behind and all around, the land undulated in varying verdant hues, with low stone walls that sank and rose along its contours. The air was moist and soft, a cut-glass blue with white clouds chugging across the sky. As we whizzed along, we glimpsed more cows: black-and-white date stamps in a green blur. There were also a fair number of palm trees, making odd, aggressive claims upon the sky. They were incongruous to my eye; after all, we weren't in the Caribbean. These unremembered palm trees were a reminder of how long it had really been.

Our destination was Annascaul, named for the "River of the Shadow" that runs near it, about halfway out to the western edge of the peninsula. At Shannon Airport, we were actually fifty-six miles west of Lough Corrib and where Annaghkeen

Castle was supposed to be, but our plan was to head west instead of east. Staying three or four nights in each town, we would more or less hug the southwest coast before traveling to Dublin, where we would spend some time, then heading straight across the middle of the country to Galway.

Ireland's southwest has three main peninsulas: Dingle, Iveragh, and Beara. They cut deep into the lower left flank of the country, comprising an extra one thousand miles of coastline where there would be only about sixty if the land were straight. These rocky promontories and bouldery beaches clamor into the Atlantic, whereas the more linear side of Ireland is on the Irish Sea. We chose Dingle, the topmost peninsula, because Beara was too far away and we had heard that Iveragh, home to the famous Ring of Kerry, was overrun with tour buses in the summer. But we were to find that Ireland almost always feels like a bigger country than it is, and underpopulated.

In Annascaul, it was hard to know that we were even in a town. There were about twelve structures, many of them pubs, and the main road seemed to have no tributary. We asked two ladies in skirts and sensible shoes for directions to our B and B, the Four Winds. "Oh yes, Kathleen O'Conner," they said, as if resuming a conversation with us from which they had only just been diverted. They directed us a half mile down the road, to a first right onto the Old Dingle Road, which we were told went "up the hill." There we'd find it.

The Four Winds, encircled by an asphalt driveway and more distantly the Slieve Mish Mountains, had a real feeling of remoteness—just what I had longed for after hectic weeks of preparation. The bungalow-style house was surrounded by green fields for miles in every direction. A car came down the narrow road once every hour or so, brushing by the overgrown bramble and broom. Kathleen O'Conner, the proprietress, knew from my earlier emails that we were from the U.S. She showed us a choice of two rooms next to each other on the parking lot, one an odd affair with a small bedroom, a full kitchen, and—up a spiral staircase—a twin bed on a glorified shelf that was an attempt at a loft. Another one had two double beds and a pull-out armchair. Picturing Emmett falling out of the loft, we chose the latter. Aside from two young backpackers staying on the other side of us, we were the only patrons.

Our body clocks, set for five hours earlier, lurched us forward. We put our bags down, weeks of preparation coming to a close. The smells, the faint sounds, the textures were exquisite, if only for the absence of anything pressing to do. The beds were decent, though the comforters had seen better days. We sprawled luxuriously, listening to the quiet. Emmett marveled at our modest bathroom, where everything was familiar to him but different—an oddly shaped, low toilet, a tiny sink and rattletrap medicine cabinet, and a square, deep tub with a seat in it, as if to accommodate a very old person. True to form, Steve had the TV working first thing. We got twelve channels through a set of rabbit ears sticking out of a brown plastic box on top of the set. Looking earnestly but perplexedly at the screen, Emmett watched Dora the Explorer, a Latina cartoon character from L.A. who teaches Spanish. However, this Dora the Explorer was speaking Gaelic where the English would have been, punctuated by the Spanish: Azure! Rosa! Verde! Azure! Rosa! Verde! To my ear, the Gaelic was unmusical and leaden. It was the first time that I can remember having heard it. I thought that despite the Irish facility with words, Gaelic, or Irish, wasn't a pretty language. Then I wondered if it wasn't just the dubbed-in voice and my uninitiated ear.

My attention drifted to the folder of poems I had brought. There were three about me—unborn, at one, and at two and three years of age. Unwittingly, my existence had opened a door into a kind of wisdom that my mother had been seeking.

Rue   1959 – one year old

Beauty of essentials; in solution—life
Perfectly turned in round wonder of the world.
Not yet you, blessed by no I, a presence curled—
In total center emanates the total light
The sun reflects in worship of an equal wife.
Her answer rises in soft ripples purled
Intoning understanding in words yet furled
Un-sentenced by thought's untrusting knife.

Violet eyes in joy must glow
Unmet by waves from a ruthless brain
Vibrating the string of its crouching bow.
Sing my child to the sound of your soul's fine strain
While I watch and for a little catch its low uprooting note
Then with my brain combine perhaps to
Smash the pane.

When I read the poem, I felt as if she were in that B and B with me and that the bond between us had never been broken. My connection to this collection of words called "Rue" was as to an underground river, warm and clear and moving and rushing and full of forward motion, a swift and endless force that had been with me always, whether I knew it or not. The poem made the surrounding facts, *born July 11, 1927—died January 28, 1972,* nonsensical. It was as if she had never died.

How gently it begins—it is sweet to enjoy a baby's innocence and joy and eyes that "must glow" in the fire of new life.

Among the images that flashed in my mind, I saw my mother still in the world—sitting opposite, reading, or perhaps toiling away on a second book (on Zen, it would have been). Or even unambitious Deborah, ordinary in a nightgown, filing her long nails, her face shiny with cream and curlers in her hair. Though I had never read it before, I remembered the meaning of the words exactly.

How clear the implication is. Though she writes that the "total center emanates the total light," time will pass, bringing unwanted thoughts, words, crushing the "soul's fine strain." A trap lies in wait, a trap that turns out to be deadly. What is it? *Why* does there have to be one? It seemed to start off so perfectly, where one got a pass, just by being a cute baby, a blank slate. A life force and nothing else.

Then, the mind and consciousness begin to tick, but they aren't illuminating, they're an obstacle. This is her poem, at age thirty-one, so my encroaching "ruthless brain" is really her ruthless brain. For her, the "sweet sound" of my soul will disappear, but she's going to listen to it for as long as she can. I will save her from self-knowledge just by existing. *Together* we will elude the "crouching bow" of the mind. For a little while, she will catch the "low uprooting note" that I provide. Then "… with my brain to combine perhaps to smash the pane."

I knew exactly what she was writing of. I could feel it between the lines. The alchemy of words in the poem called "Rue" made that facet of her character, *our* characters, jump to life. I knew that restlessness, that need for the absolute. "The pane" is a sheet of glass between her and a greater, longed-for truth. The pane is the limits of consciousness. A diorama that she wanted to smash.

I remembered a friend of hers telling me after she died about a fantasy of my mother's. The setting is an antique shop, with shelves of delicate chinaware, clocks, jewelry, crystal, precious figurines. The fantasy is what she is allowed to do—destroy everything in the shop. She can lay it to waste. It will be absolutely real, and she can choose her weapon: Baseball bat? Hammer? Axe? She can do it piece by piece or finish the job in five minutes, and no one will hear, no one will care, and most importantly, no one will judge her. Of the journey that took us across the ocean to Ireland in 1965, she wrote in *Annaghkeen:* "*I looked out of the porthole, first at the water spinning by in white swirls and streaks, and then at the sky, holding a wisp of Milky Way with here and there dull patches of stars. I thought of God sitting smugly up there, having made sentient life. Even as a child I was angry with him, so angry.*"

Within that pool of anger, I grew up. I was "the wise one" at three, four, five years old, but not because I had any wisdom. Worst of all, as I grew older the benevolent light of innocence lessened, along with the perceived wisdom. The more I knew, the more power I lost; and the more depressed she was, the more depressed I was. My increasing knowledge seemed to damage both of us. I saw the light of interest begin to fade in her eyes, and I felt it personally. As a conduit to philosophical clarity, I had been perfect, and now I was a disappointment.

I also worried about my mother; I felt her fragility, deep inside myself. I had the same fragility, but it was stuffed away behind a shell that toughened as I got older. By the age of ten, I was steeped in cynicism, a result of my mother's minute-to-minute existential bewilderment. I was shaped to some degree by my own contempt for it and for her. I thought, how naïve, how *really* innocent one has to be to wonder as hard as she did. My response was to not be innocent anymore, to protect myself from her chronic expectation that at some point answers would be furnished. In those years, for me, the world and all the happenings in it began to skew slightly but irreversibly toward the absurd. From my standpoint, "answers" were temporary flights of fancy, as flimsy as clouds in the sky. My parents so obviously didn't have any of them.

At the same time, another part of me loved her for it—felt protective of the tender spot within her that prevented her from toughening up and just getting on with it the way other people did. As much as I felt it a burden, I was also its defender. I felt, I knew, how unique it was to *not* be able to construct the usual defenses, the fixations of the well-adjusted (and not so well-adjusted): the money, ambition, romantic obsession, sex, drugs, art, and power through which people imposed some sort of order upon their lives to shield them from what might cause too much wonder and fear. How remarkable it was, she was, to remain translucent and unguarded, to have hope enough for life that she could not relinquish the belief that somewhere in the interstices of the universal mind, or even in the violet eyes of a baby, there was a skeleton key. If I could have wrapped my whole self around it and her, I would have, just to make sure the world in all of its insistent focus on the ordinary and humdrum could not destroy it.

I set aside the folder, pushing sleep away. Severely jet-lagged, I wobbled onto the asphalt driveway. My mission was to smoke, away from my family, the one cigarette I allowed myself per day. Punctuated by pots of bright pansies and geraniums, the driveway seemed to be the proud focal point of the B and B, with most of the windows looking out onto it. If this were the U.S., the water would be visible from every possible angle. The perplexing orientation of the building depicted the casual relationship the Irish have with the natural beauty of their country. Maybe the O'Conners didn't want to gaze off into the vast sea on the other side. Maybe they wanted the finiteness of the road, their driveway, and the small, rounded foothills and fields to greet them in the mornings. Having recently been taken up with so much eternity, I sort of understood it.

On the other side, Dingle Bay rose high and gray under a canopy of weeping, dripping clouds. Smells were intensified in the rain: grass, cow dung, salt from the sea, wet stone, flower and bramble—deeply familiar in a way that only impressions from childhood can be. While not actually willing *Annaghkeen* to the present, it perforated the scene, along with the memory of my mother.

At home in recent years, whenever the subject of my mother came up, the observations of others were wooden and furtive, clunking to a quick stop. I could see that everyone felt this way—it's over, nothing more to add to the story. The exceptions were a few of her closest friends, and my father, whose face softened when speaking of her. Sometimes. At other times he got it wrong. Once, he told me a long story about his first wife Patsy, not realizing until the end that I wasn't related to her. His story stammered to a halt, as it dawned on him that the complexity of his past had exceeded even his own grasp.

In the pace of ordinary time, it was sometimes impossible for me to remember my mother's qualities. I had begun having trouble remembering that warm look that she'd get in her eyes when pleased with me—that particular way of being pleased that almost no one else could inspire as far as I could tell except my brother Alex. A smile that said, "I adore you and approve of every inch of you, no matter what." I knew that to forget was natural and as it should be. She had been gone a long time. To try to force her to life could only make her more of a caricature, an animated doll, than she had already become.

The possible irrelevancy of my efforts had come to my attention again while setting up this trip. I emailed the Duffys, a family that my mother had written about in the book. They were owners of a hardware store in Headford near Annagh-keen, and I found them on the internet. I was hoping to find something about lodging in the area and also connect with them. I thought I was writing to the wife, Josephine. I wrote a more candid sort of letter than I would have to a man. I then received this reply:

"Your email just came through. You have got me mixed up. I am Kevin—husband of Josephine!! I was sorry to hear your mother had died. Pity she cannot come this time. But we must not think too much about these matters. Regards, Kevin."

How right he was, I thought. *We must not think too much about these matters.* Get a life, said Kevin Duffy. My mother would have wanted me to get a life. But not too much of one. Though I had only the distant example of her wistful, violet-eyed beauty and hip bookishness (direct advice was never given), I had the sense that if she were here, and I was a rich, high-functioning, terribly effective type with a big job and lots of kids—the sort of person who had no time for poetry—she wouldn't have been able to relate to me at all.

As I crossed the Four Winds garden, I thought about this and realized that because I hadn't known her as an adult, or what made her happy (not very much), I had gone through life making the smallest imprint possible out of respect for her extremely nonfunctional state of being (dead). I never wanted to rebel too much against that irrefutably insensate quality she had suddenly assumed, in total, in late January of 1972. To begin with, it wasn't an even match. All the arguments we had had—and there were quite a few—I had won by default, just by being the last one standing. What could she say about anything I did? Nothing. Her comments, her views, were in the simple past tense; a static pile that would never be added to. I had to respect that. She changed, from one day to the next, one hour to the next, even one minute to the next, from an all-encompassing presence to a suppositional one: a series of attributes only. She was as nonfunctioning as a person could be. She was a pile of ashes. So what right did I have to go gallivanting around, functioning everywhere? I was repelled by the idea, not to mention frightened. Death had also whacked down her second husband, Clement Pollock, two months after she died. (Pollock was my biological father. I barely knew him, having begun living with my adoptive father Peter at the age of two.) I didn't want to piss off death itself by not respecting it. I didn't want to put up any red flags for death to notice and say, "Got rid of those two, and here's another, from the same seed. Let's clean this up for good." For years I resisted any kind of functioning at all, cutting classes at every opportunity, smoking a lot of pot, scraping through years of schooling, learning the bare minimum that I would need to pass, and sometimes not even that.

After she died, I found a few cashmere sweaters of hers folded into a stack and left on the bed by Mary Wheelwright, my father's sister. For years I'd bury my nose in them for the smell of her, which made the centers of my brain light up like a starry night. One of them, salmon-colored with black and white speckles like a tern's egg, kept her particular scent for a long time: a mix of Joy perfume, the setting lotion she used with her curlers to keep the frizz out of her hair, mothballs, and coffee if it was the morning. I'd recall the feel of her, always taller than me at 5'6", with a slim waist and arms that she accentuated with wool skirts and tops that were sometimes rough under my fingers. Because of the scouring cold of the east end of Long Island, we both wore a lot of wool. She was also making up for lost time, having never been able to wear wool as a young person because of the eczema that still afflicted her from time to time. When we hugged, which we did often, her tickly soft arms felt as though they wrapped around me twice, so warm were they. Her hands were long-fingered and elegant, always manicured an opaque beige or shell-pink color that went with the neutral hues of the sweaters. Her flat waist flared out to wide hips and thighs that were jiggly, pressing her skirt, usually tweed, out to a little peak on each side. After breastfeeding two children, she still had small round breasts, with pointy nipples like pencil erasers, that she declined to contain with a bra, to the delight of almost every straight man she ever talked to. I would rest my head between them, feeling protected and sometimes forgiven and in the clear after a fight. By the age of five, I knew that the reprieve was always temporary. As I grew older, I began to realize that we were in a storm. The union of her and me, body, mind, and soul, was a way to get through the storm. I began to realize that amid those hard blowing winds I was more stable. She was looking for something, some sort of perfection that continually eluded her. I feared she'd never find it.

The soft drizzle was now deepening the slate gray of the sea. I trod off past the dripping bramble on either side of the road, which gave way on one side to stony fields with cows and sheep, and on the other to acres of more ferns and waist-high grasses, thinning a bit toward the worn old hills. There was the smell of cow "pies" and heather, while damp lichen maps traced the bigger boulders in the fields. I stopped and looked across one field in particular, walking to a wall that rang a distant echo of memory; its oblong granite shapes fitted together perfectly. I was once small enough to be almost eye to eye with walls just like it; they were another "me," their capstones friendly at shoulder level.

Was I an imposter, nudging into the deep past? Was it wise

to be after the dreams of someone else? Feeling the familiar pull of the poem called "Rue," I wanted the same perfect union that she did, where boundaries between me and the "other" were dissolved. After all, it was supposed to *begin* with me. I wanted it then; I want it still. A glimpse, a miracle, if not every day, often. Without it for too long, problems set in. Life becomes tasteless, and I am unmoored. Because of her, I want too much. I have always known that my mother's world and mine were dangerously intertwined.

My mother's generation was the last that was brought up to believe in God. She too had been indoctrinated with an expectation—these rules were woven into the fabric of each and every day—that there is a greater power, there is ultimate knowledge, there is an authority. God in the sky will redeem one, will make all one's decisions. God is in one's self, waiting to be discovered. In order to find Him, one must bow one's head. One must surrender to the existing structure, what is already in place. And it was at this point that my mother bolted. She would have to find her own different way. Not on an established path, not dictated to her, or taught in a lesson, or imposed upon her by a church, her parents, St. Louis, or any man.

I was on the same road in Ireland, looking for some sort of revelation. The difference between us is I don't expect it. In fact, perfect illumination seems to come when I least expect it. I have no active hopes for nirvana or the last best wisdom. Instead, I play a game. It's called let's see something marvelous and forget about adulthood and reality and the endlessness of time and space. Or the finiteness of time and space—whatever it is that we can't understand. Let's time-hop. Let's lose ourselves. Let's immerse ourselves in something incredible and get so wrapped up in it we can't remember the boundaries between the outside and the inside, and we are eternal, even for a moment. I traced a wet lichen flower with my finger. Instead of coming from overhead, the rain was all around me warmly, down to the ground. At the foot of a stone, Queen Anne's lace drooped with the wet, amid tufts of wild green.

Real Life

I have thought that when my children are grown I would like to enter a monastery. P thinks too of such things. Unlike Count Axel and Sara who killed themselves saying, "Let our servants do our living for us," we will let who will live Real Life while we submit to strange disciplines behind monastic walls.

It is the illusion of choice that has baffled me. When I truly remember there is none I will again be cheerful.

By day three at the Four Winds, I found myself surprisingly attached to the mediocre breakfast: scrambled eggs, white and black sausage, under-ripe fried tomatoes, sautéed mushrooms, orange juice that Emmett wouldn't drink, grapefruit juice, pallid and undersalted oatmeal, a selection of cold cereals, weak coffee that Steve wouldn't drink, and tea that was a travesty—a tea bag floating in a metal canister pot like a dead body in the Hudson. If the O'Conners once cared about return business, they certainly didn't anymore.

Our plan was to partake of the breakfast every morning and scrape through the rest of the day on snacks from the grocery, mainly because the dollar was so low against the euro. Kathleen told us that we should try the South Pole Inn in Annascaul, which was opened by the town's most notable son, Tom Crean, an explorer who was on the first British expeditions to the Antarctic. Yesterday, we went in and looked at the menu. It was completely out of our league.

We chewed silently, the new day coming upon us all at the same time. The two peaks behind the Four Winds lightened in the sun, and the bay slowly glossed over with tinsel. Despite the overall lack of quality, it had been lovely to have breakfast together, without cell phones, newspapers, multiple computers, someone having to go somewhere or get up for something. Steve and Emmett liked the sausages and bacon, Emmett clamoring for the crispiest ones at the buffet. I liked the grapefruit slices and the toast. The butter, fresh from its little pack with a clover on it, was the most delicious I'd ever tasted.

I thought of my mother's longing, frequently expressed in *Annaghkeen*, to live in hotels. As a child, her family had a nanny, a cook, a housekeeper, and a gardener. On Thursdays, the cook's night off, her mother made macaroni and cheese, the only dish she knew. By the time my mother married Peter, she could cook two dishes: beef bourguignon and borscht. Like her mother, she would never clean.

There weren't many domestics for hire on the East End of Long Island, so at any given time we had one live-in person from the Caribbean to cook, clean, and babysit—they were always stretched to the limit. There was sweet religious Celia, stern religious Agnes, unhappy Amelia, and mild, melancholic Frances, who took care of baby Alex at home in New York while we were in Ireland. I drove them all crazy, they said, except for Celia. They occupied a small room up a spiral staircase behind the kitchen, none for very long. Celia later told me that it was a lonely life all the way out on the end of Long Island in the freezing winters with no car of their own. My mother wouldn't have known how to make them comfortable even had she thought of it. She saw them mainly as independent entities from an agency, whose needs should be met by a weekly check. So they came and went, came and went. To my mother, they were interchangeable, summoned to the dining room by a quaint holdover from my parents' era: the dinner bell. Even by sixties standards, this ritual was absurd. I remember the tinkling sounds of it in the quiet, Amelia or Agnes or Celia tending to us awkwardly; the strain between my parents, the echoes of a void, of *absolutely nothing* in the house besides that dinner bell, made me tense too, and I would want desperately to fill the space. So I overflowed, heightening the tension with my childish prattle, which was considered the worst of all possible things: phony. Soon I found myself getting served a solitary, separate dinner in the kitchen by one of the maids well before my parents ate. These dinners (cold noodles, warmed-over burgers, tepid milk) tasted of everyone's disapproval.

The problem might well have been reality, the life that they were living, and consequently, I was living through them. Throughout *Annaghkeen*, my mother refers to what she calls "Real Life." There is prosaic, ugly Real Life, the opposite of an earlier held ideal of elegance and a light and sweet enjoyment. Real Life is routine, obligations, and maddeningly silent dinners. Real Life is *right now*, at home, far away from the fantasy life of a hotel, where everything is silently done for you. Real Life is modern, brutish, and funny, driving so fast into the future it can barely keep up with itself. Certainly, almost no one in the house could keep up with it, except for my father, who mainly ignored it.

Once we had moved into the Sagaponack house with my father, my mother would sometimes float in a queenly way around the bedroom in her nightie, miming a particular architectural feature she had coveted: arched "Lady Godiva" windows she had seen in the movies, windows that could open out with a flick of her wrist, while flinging her arms wide to embrace another glorious, perfect day. I would giggle at the silliness of her, flouncing around the room, a false smile affixed to her face, opening these imaginary windows and beaming out over a lawn browning in the cold. It was the opening scene from a thirties movie, the point at which the fascinating tale began. Or it could have been the closing scene, where the heroine, having struggled through great trials, has finally met her prince and set up house with him, beginning their fairy tale life together.

Then, stooping and mock grumpy, she'd labor over what she actually had: a husband who was gone a lot of the time, housekeepers who wouldn't stay, children she found unmanageable, and eleven casement windows that wound around two sides of the bedroom. Leaning down to grasp the spindle handles, she'd open them one by one with a grimace, saying, "Crank, crank, crank . . ."—a task that took between three and seven minutes, depending on how ambitious she was feeling. This was the abhorred, hysterically funny Real Life, where the strip of film in the projector has gotten tangled up, and the movie has stopped dead.

Sometimes the different sides of things weren't so funny. (And there were *always* different sides.) By marriage number three, she was too sophisticated to admit to anyone that she had hoped for the proverbial happy ending, but *I* knew that she had at least wanted to feel as though she had landed, that *we* had landed, in the right place. This was going to be mostly impossible. My father had affairs while he was gone, and sometimes right under her nose, because that's what his father did, and what he felt he had a right to. Once, when getting ready to go out for a dinner party, a ritual that always took at least one hour, she looked at me, frosted pink lipstick in hand, and said, "It's all cocks and cunts." I was about ten years old and felt gutted by these words. One entire area of life that I had some hopes for, *romantic love*, was portrayed as some sort of ugly joke.

That was well after Ireland when we were all older and somewhat weary. Angered by Peter and bored with the game, she was bitter as she took the usual care over her appearance, buying fashionable clothes, going to the beauty parlor to have the gray taken out. "I do it all," she'd say, surrounded by the detritus of her efforts: the heat roller case, the makeup, the garters, the stockings, bottles of nail polish, scent (Joy and 4711), the lingerie, shopping bags from Paraphernalia and Bonwit Teller, the rows of high heels, the close-fitting winter shifts, and the cotton summer dresses rustling in the closet, waiting to be enlivened. I loved watching her get ready for the evening, admiring how she could turn herself out. But no matter how fabulous the result, there was no joy in it for her. It was a job she felt tied to, and she did it grudgingly. She had her own work, but it was my father who had the freedom and power, and most of all the satisfaction of following his inclinations. Though his were mainly hidden, it's safe to say that her needs were not as simply dispatched. He was focused on his work, and he was a master at compartmentalization. She was different. To begin with, she was female. Her affairs were few, retaliatory, and halfhearted.

Looking back, I can't help but admire her unique approach to what were garden variety problems. Primping and shopping seemed to be part of her role as wife, which matured later into a belief that her *authentic self* was completely separate from afternoons spent at Elizabeth Arden covered with goop. It began as a pseudofeminist idea and went on from there. It was around this time that her inquiry into the nature of life and consciousness got more serious. It centered around the question: What was embellishment and what was truth? What of *herself* was true, and by extension, of anyone else? Was she "the beauty," an object, a muse? Was she then "the betrayed?" (She would have hated that, not for the hurt of it so much as the reduced standing, the ridiculousness.) What of *him* was true and could be depended on? Did he love her? Did he need her? In the era of easy divorce, what of their marriage was not temporary? Did they really need each other, after all?

When he was home, his first love was whatever book he was working on, and he was remote and irritable a lot of the time. When he was gone, she was alone and angry. Her dissatisfaction strung us between two poles: a romantic fantasy from girlhood, and its counterpoint—Real Life. The fairytale and the commonplace. The coveted, closely held vision, and the reality. The former was full of lightness, air, and promise, and the latter was harsh, hard, and ridiculous. The humor helped to get through the days, but it was unable to fix the underlying disappointment.

To the outward eye, our household looked prosperous and happy. His reviews were good, his books were selling, and there was an air of recently gained, substantial success. Deborah and Peter became well-connected in the New York literary and art scene. Editors, agents, publishers, art-world luminaries, and literary stars came through for dinners and cocktail parties, almost always with that peculiar calling card that was de rigueur in those circles in the sixties and early seventies—the outrageous story of inebriation and/or domestic failure. The sympathetic, bumbling protagonist was always male, always funny, and mirthfully forgiven for losing control of themselves and/or the location of their families. Everyone understood that the onus and weight of making art or writing books far outweighed such concerns. The wives went along with the hilarity, having not yet begun to understand the implications. Those who did understand were tempered by the surprisingly warm glow of celebrity and believed in the sacrifices necessary to great art. Everyone was very young. My mother put a smile on her face and laughed along because they *were* funny and surprisingly touching, these stories of bungling buffoons at the mercy of their talent and their love and need of women. Softened as she was by the joke, on them and on herself, the laughter didn't fix it. In fact, the laughter excused it, which made it worse to laugh along, to genuinely find it funny. There was still the morning ahead, cranking open those windows, alone. The living room studded with half-empty highball glasses and crumpled napkins. A grumpy housekeeper hiding in the room above the kitchen. Real Life at home was not a happy place. The job of maintaining a false exterior fell mainly to her, which created an ever-sharper divide between her and my father.

Conversely, an *idealized* version of Real Life was threaded throughout our lives. It was in my father's books and in objects from his travels—an actual shrunken head, American Indian baskets and pots, a collection of axes from New Guinea, woven baskets and earthen pots from Africa that decorated the house. *This* Real Life was had and enjoyed by the indigenous, the poor, even the middle class, who were by necessity taken up with practical concerns. These Real Lives were defined by the simplicity of having few choices or none, which ordained them, in my parents' view, with a kind of mystical grace. The modern world might learn from them. *We* might learn from them. Once, in Africa, my mother pointed out to me the exquisite form of a Masai warrior's wife whom my father had spotted. The woman was tall and slender against a hot orange sun, her baby slung to her front as she tended a herd of cattle. My mother studied her, sure of the woman's semi-holy state of being, her life pared to the slimmest essentials, framed by the dramatic splendor of an African sunset.

Ireland afforded many more opportunities to see the beauty of simple living. Though my mother rarely did laundry, and never by hand, the sight of a farm woman's laundry was an opportunity for poetry. In this lovely passage, she has seen a wife taking wet clothes across the road to the shrubbery to dry:

Clean clothes spread on bushes are pleasant, yet less thrilling than laundry hung out on a line: touching symbols of human shapes strung side by side, jumping, snapping in a breeze, or—more eloquent—quiet on a windless day. I love a whole white line of children's cotton underpants, especially when an orderly wife has hung them in expanding sizes. Rows of diapers are strangely not monotonous; one following another, a simple statement of the succession of time. Shirts, neckless, held by the shoulders, pants swung by the cuffs, a union suit hung upside down, empty, flexible; brassieres bold next to blue jeans, mothers and sons in startling intimacy, pristine. Slips are sad, vulnerable, trifling. Overalls are cheerful; they speak of men coming hungry to the table.

Each clean diaper marks the slow passing days of babyhood, a man's suit (without the man) is flexible, mothers and sons can be guiltlessly close, though the things of the woman are sad and trifling. The overalls are cheerful because hunger is sharp, the meal is deserved. The meal seems to be deserved mostly by the men; the woman is invisible but for the food she provides and the order she creates on the line. She doesn't seem to have much fun, though the result is beautiful and poetic:

Real Life has been done for another day and will continue. It must, the family depends upon it, and each other. The thing that holds Real Life together is need. There are few choices; they must stay together.

Real Life in Ireland often happened on farms:

Beautiful farms, a house under trees, the straight line of shed shapes becomes a village across the yard strewn with machines and white chickens . . . I don't want to be a farmer, I just want to be around farms.

And one time, our VW got caught in the outflow from a church in Headford:

. . . we watched while they flowed around us in the narrow street. They were stylishly dressed and many of the women and girls were beautiful . . . These women, dressed so well, had a seductive sense of themselves. So too have the countrymen of Ireland, perhaps from a sense of themselves so close to the beasts and the soil. Housework does not make vivid the female, though if she go to the field or the farm yard, she is enhanced.

Their seductive power comes from their involvement with each other and their collective interest, farming. Their roles are simple and proscribed, limited by what is available to them. Restricted by convention, they are made beautiful. The warrior's wife, the laundress, and the farmers were examples of the other, romantic side of Real Life. In a natural state of immersion, at one with their surroundings, they have purpose. They belong. They have a specific contentment that she believed was smothered in *her* life under layers of frustrating obfuscation, as well as her inability to be "simple enough." Her problem, she said, was an abundance of choice. Her problem was also the abundance of choices of everyone around her, especially my father.

She did love the idea of doing useful, practical things, and God knows she tried. Once, inspired by Frances Hodgson Burnett's *A Secret Garden*, she spent weeks planting a garden in a plot near our barn that was surrounded by twelve-foot-high privet because it looked just like the garden in the book. Everything died for lack of sun, an outcome that made her laugh at herself for years, but not without a certain sadness, because she had really made an effort. The idea of Burnett's dormant roses and smothered snowdrops finding new life was magical to her, but the simple alchemy of sun, water, and nutrition proved impossible. She just didn't have the knack.

Then there was a cooking phase, where she took time out from her reading and writing to attempt a few experiments in the kitchen. One afternoon, she had a beef bourguignon simmering on the stove for a dinner party. Because there wasn't much food in the house, I was often hungry as a child, resorting to eating, at times, dog food. I distinctly remember the brand: Alpo Meatballs. I wouldn't go for the other, mushy stuff. But if a can of Alpo Meatballs was left on top of the breakfront, I'd sometimes grab a few bites because there was hardly any food in the refrigerator, and I was not allowed to snack because of my weight. Another option was to get into the jars of rum baba in the pantry when the maid wasn't in the kitchen. Though the rum in them wasn't tasty, I overlooked it for the sake of the round yellow cakes soaked in sugar. The rum baba left me with a strange buzzing feeling and slightly sick from the alcohol.

On the day of the dinner party, the beef bourguignon, a significant step up from Alpo, was irresistible. I spent the entire afternoon running back and forth from my room at the other end of the house with a demitasse spoon, taking a bite at a time, not realizing how many trips I had made. When she came down from her study and saw the depleted dish, she broke down and cried because she had four people coming for dinner, an enterprise that already intimidated her. She was furious at me for days, which was a long time for her to be angry. I remember feeling terribly sorry. I knew she was angry because the day she had spent cooking felt pointless to her. For me to eat the stew piled stupidity on top of wasted time, more than doubling the loss. To her, cooking felt like running in place, a redundant exercise where material for consumption was provided, used, and expelled. Her frustration was not *getting anywhere* with it. Like coal shoveled into a furnace, food was just fuel that came out of the other end—the whole of human experience not any less perplexing for it, and certainly more frustrating.

Her rejection of domestic enterprise wasn't absolute. There was wistfulness, a way that she looked at "homemaking" out of the corner of her eye. When she wasn't immersed in study or Zen, she felt herself a failure for having been married three times by the age of thirty-one. After all, she hadn't turned out to be the ideal woman that it had been drummed into her mind she should be. She wasn't presiding over stacks of folded laundry or standing at the front door to greet her family with a freshly baked pie. So now and then she'd get a wild idea and try her own version of homemaking. She tried making bread but could not get the loaf to rise. She made yogurt (then called yoghurt) in four little glass cups kept lukewarm in a device on the kitchen counter (impossible to screw up). She tried knitting: I still have the scarf, a red, bumpy little scrap with a blue anchor sewn on haphazardly—one of my dearest possessions. She did needlepoint (half a canvas in purple and yellow, a Zen proverb) and Japanese Sumi painting. She blew out Easter eggs with her friend, Danish beauty Merete Galesi, and painted brown branches with blue flowers on them. Drawn to the power of minimalism, she wanted to be the woman who lovingly gardened, who farmed and made things, someone who was content with simplicity.

The romanticized version of Real Life held up—there in the Irish farmers moving around the car like a school of fish (in which my parents sat isolated), and in the graceful form of the Masai woman on the African plain. Later, the curios from my father's expeditions accumulated: a set of elegant spears used by New Guineans to defend territories, hand-beaded American Indian vests, intricately painted Inca pots. During the *Annaghkeen* summer and beyond, simplicity as a solution began to metamorphose into a fantasy of monastic life. On a visit to Mount Melleray Abbey, a monastery in the Knockmealdown Mountains, my parents stayed overnight, participating in a program where guests were allowed to observe the rituals along with the monks. In regard to what would be her eventual devotion, she wrote:

I would like to enter a monastery . . . though of what kind I cannot know; but were I able to take vows to Christian realities, I could not live solely among women, an aesthetic imbalance.

So she would take my father along. They would find that place where, limited by the conventions of religion, they would themselves be made simple enough for the idealized Real Life, or for the grittiness of the other "real" Real Life, or some amalgam of the two. Would children have a place there? They might, but only if they left their childish nature behind. Children are loud and needy, and they change all the time—as soon as you've adjusted to one phase, there's a transformation. My parents found them lovable and interesting but didn't really believe they had much *effect* on children past the age of twelve or so, while harboring deep and hopeless regrets about them. Better to have the children at least a half mile from the monastery, in a field, playing prettily under a large, sheltering tree. Real Life, but not too real.

For me, Real Life is just where I am. It is often more real to me on the road, traveling, than at any other point. When I'm home, supposedly immersed in "real" Real Life, it can have the quality of a videotape loop. That is why I love to travel. The colors and sounds and sights are a film I watch closely for the detail that tells, the fragment that falls into place. I pull the surroundings in, a taste of this, a bit of that; I wonder at every person that walks by, wonder how they feel about where they live, and yet by the time the sun has begun its descent from the sky's apex, I already know. A new self is created. I am Italian in Italy and black in Philadelphia. In New York, on the day of the Puerto Rican parade, I'm Puerto Rican. In Amsterdam, I'm one of those folk on a bike, zipping down a canal after work, blonde tresses aloft in the wind. To be a chameleon trying on cultures is my favorite part.

Ireland, especially, is a place of vivid reimagining for me. Having walked every day for miles around our adopted bungalow, I felt Irish again, as though I hadn't really ever left this island. We picked wildflowers into small bouquets for the room, we heard the cows lowing when we awoke, we roamed unchecked into the worn green hills. It seemed as though not all that much had changed. How much of my mother was still here: the closely held fairy tale, Real Life gritty and difficult, Real Life beautiful and perfect, all as true as if she were right beside me, funny and warm, and laughing, as she often did, at her own situation. Then she would think—it isn't that funny, things are not right, not at all, and tears quickly come, dropping from the ends of her long dark lashes. Through a thin cashmere sweater, she radiates the heat of a young person. She's combing my hair and hasn't gotten the tangles out. She's reading the last chapter of Alan Watts's *The Wisdom of Insecurity*, plucking gently at her eyebrow in concentration. She's writing a poem and hasn't finished all of her meticulous, painstaking edits. She's making borscht and has forgotten the sour cream (or has dropped her spoon and left the kitchen, sick of making borscht).

There is no older Deborah, calmed-down Deborah, no grounded Deborah, no Deborah who finally found home. No Deborah who found a Real Life of any variety to which she could meaningfully adhere. There's no effervescent Deborah, gone for a walk on a sharp winter day after finishing her latest book. There's no mellowed Deborah, her fashion sense gone happily astray, watching the midafternoon news with a cat on her lap. She's midsentence, as flattened as a paper doll under the weight of everything that had to move forward. Now there are no more irritating alternatives to bother her, no Real Life problems, no real life either. No life at all. After a period of reflection under this huge pile of stuff, she's not happy. She's not happy and she hasn't been for years and years, though she has had to put a good face on it (along with my father, and me, and all the Zen people, and all her friends and relatives), though she puts on a pretty good show, gazing out from her memorial pamphlet with its portrait of her beautiful face, its pallor telling of her recent diagnosis, her eyes soulful and deep, the picture ringed with a slash of black ink from a Sumi painter's brush, deep and absolute.

Tinkers

North of Galway, on the road to Cong
Beyond all parishes, in bare rain plains of peat
The tinker fires, all the road along

I will go and be a tinker, says the child
Seeing ponies and bright caravans and bare brown feet

And who would not?
In weather fair and wild
To be so near the sky, and sing one's
song
If life were left from scavenging
For the bent pot.

~Peter Matthiessen

The Dingle Peninsula is like a giant log in the sea, and one always has the sense of its slope toward it, along with a land-shaped breeze that comes bouncing across from the ocean on the other side. About two-thirds down the peninsula, the center road veers toward the coast and Dingle town. As we went, we noticed a tingly brine on the wind. Following our noses, we turned onto an unmarked road so narrow that it was hard to imagine two cars on it. I was to later find that on this sort of lane cars pull over and nose into a field to let you pass, or go screaming by. The speed at which they make the judgment of who will yield and who will pass is astounding.

Fortunately, no one was coming our way. We crept along, meadow brome and sedge grass as high as the car windows, like a green tunnel. Steve had a terrible headache from not being able to attain his usual caffeine blood level at the Four Winds. For him, the whir of the grinder is the sacred sound that signals the start of each day. As it is for most recovered alcoholics, coffee is heavy with symbolism. A&P is the brand of choice, or "Demon Roast," a dense, sharp brew we can only get in New Hampshire. I was hoping for better at our next B and B, though Steve, ever the pessimist, declared that the coffee would be dismal at any place we stayed. I was beginning to regret not having brought one of those traveling espresso kits and at least two pounds to get us to Dublin, where I was sure they must have decent coffee.

Emmett needed to pee. Even in those grasses he was shy. So we opened two car doors he could stand between, while Steve and I laid the map out on the hood of the car. He was worried that we were on private land. I theorized that if we were, the piece was so big that it would hardly matter. Weren't these walkers in the British Isles always on somebody else's property? Yes, but we were driving, not walking, he pointed out, and added, while referring to the dysfunctional map, that there was no way to tell where we actually *were*. We were on an *adventure*, I said, as we piled back into the car. Around another bend, we came upon a herd of at least twenty sheep clogging the road. Like us, they were packed tight in, unable to escape into the tall grasses. We bumped along, surrounded by their bleats and twiddling black ears and intimations of mild panic. Emmett, hanging from the window as we crept along, was delighted. A few minutes later, the grasses gave way to a field of heather, where the sheep scattered like lazy rocking horses.

At the foot of the slope, looking out over the glittering expanse of Dingle Bay, we saw a trailer park, a big one. Where we live, trailer parks are eyesores, hidden away in the scrub-pine woods. They're the cheapest form of housing and are considered the last resort, just before having no home at all. This group of about fifteen was on a lonely shallow bluff, with nothing around it but the wide blue sea and big sky. Dwarfed by the scale of it all, the effect was one of cheerful self-depreciation, as if the owners, whoever they were, had wanted things to stay just this way.

As we approached, we noticed a peculiarity about the place. But for the squawk of a gull and the intermittent rustle of wind, it was dead quiet. It was so still that we didn't dare speak. With no sign of an inhabitant, we were encouraged in our snooping. I find that the absence of people can be a conduit to understanding them, just like a ghost town can tell you something. With no eyes peering from doorways, no lifted curtains, even Steve was pulled in and led the way. As we broached the pathway between two of the trailers, there was a nearness about the place; it had a ring of the familiar, though I couldn't think why. It wasn't a town, it wasn't a village; it was sort of a settlement, with most of the trailers on concrete blocks, looking as though they hadn't been moved in a long while.

Well-trampled bare earth surrounded most, with plastic toys strewn about. They were parked in a kind of fan pattern on the bluff, each with its biggest window positioned toward the sea for a scrap of view. Some were blocked entirely but still parked at a hopeful angle, as though the neighboring one might disappear one day. Some were quite dilapidated and run down. We strolled along, taking it in, expecting someone—anyone. Water dripped from outside taps. Kitchen windows displayed bottles of dishwashing liquid, soup cans, and boxes of crackers. A jury-rigged porch with a clothesline hung on the ocean side of one, laundry flapping in the breeze.

We wondered if these were unoccupied vacation spots, or perhaps interim housing for people without homes. Then it occurred to me—they might be tinkers. The place reminded me of the camps, well-documented in *Annaghkeen*, that we had often seen by the roadside in the sixties. I knew for a fact that starting in 1963, the Irish government had been trying to "settle" this ancient wandering culture—an effort that began with giving them trailers to live in. The complaint was and is that their wandering way of life caused them to camp on private land, and the other was that they were thieves and criminals. In 1965, my mother wrote:

Two painted wagons, green with gay yellow scrollwork, are parked off the pavement. Between them a canvas is thrown over wooden hoops making a third shelter. Things they can sell sit under the open sky, pieces of wood, toilets lying on their side, an old chassis. Across the road the wash is spread on the hawthorn bushes to dry, giving it the strange rage of blossoms.

Tinkers were tinsmiths (hence the name) and horse traders who went from town to town. Though they provided many services, they were considered untrustworthy or worse. They still are. (When we have asked about them on our travels, we have mostly been met with frowns. The "settled Irish" still think of them as a troublesome nuisance.) Historically, they were believed to be descended from the families uprooted by Cromwell's "ethnic cleansing" policy and/or families who became homeless in the 1845 famine. Another theory is that they were a hybrid offshoot of Europe's Romani/Gypsy population. A recent genetic study has shown that those theories are false and that the Traveller population is genetically distinct from both Roma/Gypsies *and* from the greater population in Ireland.[1] Travellers are *anciently* Irish, but because of a resistance to intermarrying with the settled population—going back at least six hundred years and possibly much longer—they are genetically separate.

Now, Travellers occupy the lowest rung of the Irish class system, as they did when we lived here in the sixties. I remember seeing their camps around Galway, the painted wagons and horses, and packs of mostly blond feral children in dirty clothes. I remember the way they looked back at us as if from a diorama, aware of a wall of glass somewhere between them and us that would under no circumstances be breached. I wanted to play with them and would have walked right in if my parents had let me. To me, the tinkers were living outside of time, and I was greatly drawn to them. I wanted to leave my family and be absorbed into that picture, to sing and hear fairy stories at night, sleep in a wagon under the stars, never stay anywhere long, and never have to brush my teeth or do homework or anything I didn't want to do. I was obsessed. Their refusal to have jobs or houses, and go day to day by their wits, was to me an ideal life.

Having been immersed in the wanderings of my own imagination, I was surprised when Steve shushed me, grabbing my arm to stop. *Listen*, he said, and I did. Shouts and cries came over the trailers, disjointed and piecemeal like lobbed tennis balls. He looked at me—*now* we'd have to explain ourselves unless we just exited the way we'd come. I was ready to agree, but Emmett danced into a grassy clearing ahead of us, the fleeting shapes of children crisscrossing our narrow view. As we got closer, we saw about twelve kids were kicking a ball around, tended only by a black and white sheepdog. Not one of them was older than ten. Like the trespassers we were, we were intensely relieved to see no adults, while thinking how strange the scene was.

I tried to get Emmett acquainted with one boy, first by asking his name. Sean's arms and legs were filmed over with soil, giving him the look of a tree nymph. He had a tight, weary face and old eyes for a child. I asked him how old he was. Eight, he said, kicking the ball our way. I asked him where his parents were, and he looked at me warily, then shrugged his shoulders. "Out," he said, giving the ball a kick to Emmett and waiting watchfully for its return, which was a long time coming. Emmett had wandered off to play with the sheepdog.

While Emmett dawdled with the dog, we walked the little lanes that trailed westward, alert for the shadow of an adult doing dishes or hanging wash on one of the laundry lines that went from trailer to trailer. It was spooky. The place really might be a Traveller camp, I said to Steve, my imagination taking over again. Sean was cagey, as if he'd been trained not to speak to us. (I had read that Travellers never write things down, they just tell stories. That's why no one knows for sure where they come from, least of all them. And they might not even care.) I squeezed a shirt and found it slightly damp. Maybe there was a fair of some kind nearby; tinkers were always at fairs, trading horses.

Back at the field, there was a leader of the games, a round-cheeked boy of around ten with a halo of black shaggy curls. He gave us a beautiful, confident smile. Very un-tinkerlike. His name was Colm. Behind him stretched the green of the clearing, the trailers, and then an emerald field looking out over the ocean. Around him was his posse, his community, his warrior tribe, some as young as four or five, and we could see that he was proud of them. A group of girls playing hopscotch wore leather lace-up shoes and tattered sweaters with dresses of worn cotton. Above them, a few clouds were poised like ships chugging toward the water.

Whether or not they were Travellers, I had a pang thinking that Emmett would never have this kind of freedom, not because we don't want to give it to him, but because we live in a very populated area with lots of cars, and because nobody else lets their kids wander so he wouldn't have anyone to play with. In the U.S., children running around alone off a remote road near the ocean with no adults anywhere could cause the arrest of the responsible parties. We pay a lot to send our children to supervised activities, where they are supposed to be protected from every type of mishap: broken bones, boredom, hurt feelings, drugs, sex, lawsuits. I've already noticed a different attitude in Ireland—that it is the rare place where children are not present, and where they are they seem to be having a much better time, like these kids in the sunshine among themselves.

The word *tinker* was first recorded in 1175, though there have been references to itinerant metal workers in Ireland since pre-Christian times.[2] They've been called *pikies, knackers* (from trading in dead or old horses bound for slaughter), and *gippos,* with *tinker* being the mildest of the lot. While Ireland slowly went from a land of colonies and tribes to a central government, the Travellers remained tribal and apart. They lived among but outside the society of villages and towns for centuries, dealing in scrap metal and kitchenware, horse breeding and trading, and dog breeding. They never partook in the centralization of power in Ireland. As the country developed into an ownership society, they were increasingly perceived as thieves and troublemakers. The changeover to the name *Travellers* came in part because of negative connotations of the word *tinker*.

A University of Belfast study says, "Travellers rarely marry a member of the settled community, and any such intermarriage would be source of terrible shame to the settled Irish family to this day. Their alterity has usually been perceived as an undesirable kind of 'differentness' in Ireland. Likewise, the Traveller community will never consider a member of the settled community who marries a Traveller one of their kind, though his/her children will be accepted as such."[3]

In, but not of. Among, but not with. That was perfect romance for my mother and is a magnet for me still. In order to satisfy her expansive curiosity, she would simply walk away and live as a nomad. No written history, no written language, yet a multicentury lineage and culture set apart. My mother wrote of the particular quality of the Travellers that galls the progress-oriented and entrances children:

The tinkers do not look gay—they simply look still; their faces enclose the intensity of their existence, are not open or curious or confused. They do not look at us. We stare at them. They are handsome under a wild look of living outdoors but not from the wildness of life. A woman has long strawberry-blond hair tied away from her shoulders. She is aristocratic-looking, handsome and simple, and has the stature of belonging.

To have no aspirations to fix anything or oneself to one spot, but to live instead with the material knowledge of constant change. To reject the idea of permanent housing and the compromise that comes with it. To choose a wandering existence, like a migrating bird. To see the system that delivers a secure and settled life for a flimsy sham, dependent on an external paradigm to which one must subscribe and conform. It isn't surprising at all that my mother was drawn to them, and I was too.

At the same time, the seduction wasn't just the completeness and wildness that a child longs for; it was in the escape—perhaps a more adult impulse. I understand the person who doesn't want to go inside and get into the coffin of their bed, which fits into the larger coffin of their house. I get the person who wants to watch the last of the sun slide over the edge of the earth every night, and never more than three nights in a row the same horizon. On the move, one is never a target. On the road, one is moving toward the future, in tandem with time's progression, instead of getting left behind. To me, the ancient, nomadic interpretation of the concept of "progress" is just as valid as the modern one, and perhaps more benign.

The settlement programs were begun a few years before the *Annaghkeen* summer, in a concerted effort to rid the roads of the tinkers' painted wagons and scruffy horses.[4] There hadn't been an increase in incidents; the settlement idea arose out of conflicting philosophies. For how could Ireland comfortably adhere to the exciting concept of a better future under the age-old gaze of a tribe living outside of time, content to remain in stasis?

Back in the clearing, the curly-haired Colm rolled the ball to Emmett and exhorted him in a thick brogue, "Kick it, kick it!" About half the kids seemed to be heading in the same direction toward one goal, made up of two shoes on the south end. We held our breath until Emmett connected his foot with the ball and sent it flying southward, which we both prayed was the right direction. Turned out not to be, but it didn't matter. The kids were fascinated by his racy American sneakers, his long hair, and his flat accent. We lay down on the grass and watched awhile.

Eventually, Emmett and I left the group behind and wandered toward the sea, while Steve checked the car. I had fantasized that the kids were tinkers of old, but it was hard to tell. I hadn't wanted to risk insulting them by asking. One thing was certain of the persons who lived in this camp: their presence, physical or otherwise, wasn't in this place. The laundry flapping in the breeze, the boondoggled furniture and grease stains in the dirt had a careless quality—this was a transient home. That is not to say that it was not happy. It was, but there was no pride of ownership. The sky stretched from one end of the low, blue-bottomed horizon, the wind accelerated, ruffling awnings, whirling eddies of candy wrappers and tissue. As we walked, rectangles of gray sea vanished behind white trailers that looked as if they too were moving.

We went on toward the water and came to a stone wall and barbed wire that enclosed a small field of no evident purpose, except to grow, in lumpy untilled earth, the greenest grass I have ever seen. Though we had some ways to go before we would get there, I was reminded, in the most intimate way, of the fields around the Annaghkeen island that were just that shade of green.

At the corner was a meandering trail, which could be accessed only by climbing over the barbed-wire wall. I hoisted Emmett over and followed him, turning this way and that, down a packed-dirt path bordered with bell heather and emerald grass, until we reached the beach. Beyond, the sea ran up shiny metal-colored flats of sand, exploding into small clouds at the shoreline.

Eventually, Steve re-joined us, probably thinking that he would lose track of us somehow. I know enough not to get out of his sight for too long, for he worries. No place to get lost though, just soft old hills and open fields rolling down to shallow, bearded bluffs. The only visible habitation was the trailers, perched over the sea like a series of shipping containers. Looking west along the coastline, I was struck by the dominance of the landscape, the jaggedness and curve of the coast all the way down to Slea Head and Great Blasket Island.

Steve said his headache was worse, and indeed he had begun to look lifeless, his face the color of sliced almonds. Why couldn't he have had three or four cups of the coffee they had at the Four Winds? I explained again that Ireland was going to be British mainly, in terms of caffeinated beverages. What about strong tea if we can find it? No to that, he said, and forget about the regular coffee here. Our only hope was to find a place that made espresso. I said that can't be true; they must have decent coffee somewhere in this country.

At a spot nestled into the dunes, we rested awhile. Thin crags of volcanic rock that jutted from the hillside reappeared at the waterline and beyond. Hollow wells, some worn smooth, some with jagged edges, provided respite for still more types of sea life: sea urchins, sea anemones, and tiny silver minnows. Emmett, shoes discarded, concentration absolute, squatted in a tidal pool, poking at sea creatures and beds of wavering sea plants. Waves burst from the rocks near him from time to time, completely unheeded. I wondered about the land all along the road that loosely followed the coast. Was it parkland? Was it private? It wouldn't be long before houses popped up all around here if it was not conserved.

We headed back through the trailer camp, saying hello and goodbye again to the pack of kids with their shrewd friendly eyes and the sheepdog. The dog hunkered down, looking ready to herd the children if necessary. Still no grown-up in sight.

Colm waved goodbye to us, as did Sean and the others. Emmett wanted to know, "Where are their mommies and daddies?" As we left that odd, wild place, we had no answer.

The Ancients

Alone, sometimes, if I am sure the door is locked, I fall upon my knees. I want to worship—something; want forgiveness—but from whom? When I was a child I asked my Catholic nurse for a rosary and kneeled beside my bed every night and said Our Fathers and Hail Marys until my knees couldn't bear it, and I went to bed wondering and sad. In summer I threw myself onto the earth and stretched out my arms to hug her and be hers, and then I sat up, unchanged and baffled with yearning.

As we pushed out onto the Dingle road again, slices of sun slanted down the hills and silvered the sea in the distance. Steve likes to travel without too much of a plan. He is a bit of a wanderer like me, though our styles are completely different. On vacation he likes to revert to his pre-responsibility days, when, living in places like Balboa, California and Tempe, Arizona, his existence was a long meander from place to place, not knowing what he was looking for until it was found. In the U.S. he still wants to drift around, and I resist because I'm afraid of mini-mall purgatory. Truth be told, he's no good with maps, and like many men, hates having to ask for directions, an often-frustrating combination. I was driving and couldn't look at a map, so we reverted to his floating-along style by default.

With Dingle Bay and the Iveragh Peninsula a constant on our left, this was the perfect place to wing it because there was nothing impeding a sense of the way forward. About two-thirds of the way down, the ring road took over, hugging the coast. The ancient Slieve Mish range rose in soft swells to the north, with an endless patchwork of stone walls that seemed to take no notice of the road we were on and just continued down to the black tumble of boulders at the foot of the land. The ocean was a deep slate blue, with nary a ship or a boat upon it. From a distance, we could see the road along the shoreline's dips and curves, falling to black boulders and cotton-white waves as still as if painted in oil.

It was on Dingle Peninsula that I first really had a sense of how the geography of Ireland determined its history. First, its small size made it susceptible to invasion; there is no inland point that is farther than fifty miles from a coast. Second, its position as the last stop in the Atlantic Ocean after England made it vulnerable and isolated. The end of Dingle, where we were headed, is the British Isles' westernmost point—if one doesn't count the Blasket Islands and a funny little McMansion-sized islet (8,400 square feet) called Rockall.

In *Annaghkeen*, my mother often throws in sentences that allude to centuries of Irish history, as if the reader would easily know the context. On page 146, she writes:

Patrick was a Roman trained in Gaul and when he came to explain the Father, the Son, and the Holy Ghost the Druidic night withdrew before the rays of a Christian day.

Roman? Druidic night? *Annaghkeen* has a scholarly tone throughout that assumes the reader has been at least as good a student of European history as my mother was or has a deep background in Christianity. It leaves the average reader like me somewhat adrift. My mother's friend Merete said that Deborah spoke eloquently and knowledgably on almost any subject. She and their mutual friend, the salonnière Muriel Oxenberg Murphy, were known for their discourse at dinner parties, outshining many of the highly learned and literary male guests. And it's true that my mother had a retentive intelligence and was reading and writing almost all of the time. As well as being a good student, she was also a product of her time, brought up in the post-depression Midwest, where religion was the backdrop. It wasn't considered strange or even questionable that her nurse told her Bible stories every night. She laughed these experiences off, but I think she was much more affected by the promise of heaven than she let on.

There was only one generation between Bishop Potter and my mother's mother, Mary Potter. Grandmother went to church, and though the family was not very religious, church was a part of everyday life in St. Louis in the fifties. I still have *The Book of Common Prayer* my grandmother gave my mother when she was twenty-three, embossed with her name in gold letters, *DEBORAH ANNE LOVE.* It is inscribed: *"Easter, 1950. What a wonderful holiday with my child Debby I always remember—Denver—Good Friday—Easter with your loving mother."* Sixteen years later, my grandmother died on her knees at her bedside at seventy-six. My mother, still angry at her for deserting the children, declined to attend her funeral, a choice my father thought she'd regret. As far as I know, she never did. Her decision is a perfect example of the absolutism that was her strength as well as her weakness. For how, with such a rigid standard, could she ever have forgiven herself?

I haven't read *The Book of Common Prayer* or the Bible, having never had any context for them. Christianity was all but abolished in our house by the time Grandmother died, which might also have had something to do with my mother's harsh decision. Consequently, Christianity has always been somewhat of a mystery to me. Steve has a strict Catholic background, and he did the same thing my parents did and left Christianity behind for Zen. Having gone to Sunday school and been confirmed, he was able to answer many of the questions I had about the Catholic Church while touring Ireland.

Luckily for me, Steve's father has a collection of history books that concentrated mainly on the last one thousand years in Ireland. I read that this scrap of land off the shoulder of what is now the United Kingdom was literally on the edge of the modern world. It was a wild and purposeful place, but always an outsider. Cultural and theological waves came to its shores, were assimilated, and were then exported again. Irish history, from about the fifth century on, is synonymous with Christianity, and these early Christians were rebels and revolutionaries. I could more clearly see now why my parents wanted to come here.

The great benefit to Ireland now is that so much of its history is still visible. Many centuries of poverty and deprivation have had one happy result; the past is largely unobscured by the destructive hand of prosperity. Stone Age dolmens, solitary standing stones, stone circles, beehive huts, and cairns are everywhere on farms and hillsides. They are among cattle and sheep, sometimes used for livestock pens; they are in towns and villages of every size, sometimes protected and sometimes not. In our traverse through Shannon, we saw, next to a busy modern bridge, a ruined castle on a riverbank—a softened, lenticular anachronism amid the hectic pace of crisscrossing cars and people.

After a short while, we whizzed by the easy-to-miss entrance to the Fahan Beehive Huts and doubled back. Dingle boasts the largest collection of beehive huts, or clocháns, anywhere in the world. Steve was interested in these, in part because learning something he doesn't know is so much a part of his enjoyment of any place. Unlike me, he remembers facts of all kinds—they frame his world. Holding tightly onto Emmett, we rested our bellies on the warm stone wall, peering over a 260-foot drop to wet black rocks and a tumultuous white sea.

After a short walk uphill, we came to five small dwellings that were exactly the shape of beehives—all made with oblong, lichen-encrusted stones. Emmett poked around looking for leprechauns, his entire top half disappearing into a hole at the base of one wall. He went into the adjoining field, where thickets of ferns, brambles, and woodbine grazed his chin. At a certain point, all we could see was his camera, waving above the profusion of green. The vegetation in Ireland grows as if it's on crack, and no more so than on this hillside, dotted into the distance with banks of sedge and buckler ferns.

These undated early huts were incredibly sturdy and are thought to have been in use for close to fifteen hundred years, to about AD 1200. It is interesting to note that most of the historic buildings in Ireland were inhabited by the poor. According to Robert Macalister, "The wooden dwellings of the wealthy classes, of which we possess gorgeous descriptions in the literature, have all decayed to nothing. These bee-hive huts could be erected rapidly and cheaply, with stones picked up on the surface of the fields; if covered on the outside with mud or sods they would be warm and dry; they were at least as comfortable as many mud cottages."[5]

Looking around, I thought of what it must have been like to weather a stormy winter night here, anchored only by this modest assemblage of stones. Their diminishment to just five is probably the result of being raided by neighbors and farmers—for these unmortared stones, selected millennia ago to fit together so perfectly, would greatly reduce the work of any farmer or neighbor needing a ready-made wall.

While poking around, we talked about the sheer ancientness of Ireland—how *old* old can really be. By the time the Celts arrived approximately twenty-five hundred years ago, Ireland was *already* a land of ancient cultures. While dominating politically, they added their matriarchal gods and deities (Angus Og, the Dagda, and Dana, the mother of all Gods) to the cultural memory, making many established sacred places of Ireland theirs too. The resultant mix was Druidism, which included the first simple written language: ogham, which can be seen on the early grave markers and upright stones. The Druid poets or "seers" were respected and feared. I loved this particular bit; these Druids were *writers*. They were thought able to predict the future, and they were the keepers of stories and legends of the past. Sometimes they were lawyers and judges, but first and foremost they were wordsmiths. Language has always been vital in Ireland, and though English was foisted upon them, it was eventually incorporated and made their own. Another reason why my parents were drawn here.

From our post at the beehive huts, we could see far away across the water the aptly named promontory of Slea Head—a slumped mass of land that looked bowed in a kind of surprise at having run into the ocean. From here, one could see why *this* was considered the end of the known world. Maybe this lonely vista deterred the Romans, or maybe, having conquered all of Europe, they just ran out of steam. In any event, after Rome invaded Britain in AD 43, they were done. They left Ireland to itself. This might have been the most definitive thing to happen to Ireland, or in this case, to not happen. Cultural pollinations continued though, from across the Irish Sea. Ireland was the last to get them and the last to let them go, which made the country into a kind of hothouse, especially in regard to Christianity.

. . . and when he came to explain the Father, the Son, and Holy Ghost the Druidic night withdrew before the rays of a Christian day.

I was surprised to discover that Patrick was a Romano-British kid who came to Ireland in the early fifth century as a slave among many slaves. Patrick's years in captivity were spent tending the flock of a Druidic high priest in County Antrim. Here he refined his vision, praying many times a day, as well as learning the Celtic tongue to add to his native Latin. Six years later, he escaped back to Britain and later returned as a missionary, spending about forty years, until his death, spreading the word of Christ in Ireland. While Rome slowly crumbled and Europe succumbed to the dark ages, the church that Patrick and other missionaries had brought blossomed and eventually flourished into the seventh and eighth centuries, which are widely considered Ireland's "Golden Age." Existing Druid/pagan myths were absorbed into the new religion without much resistance, but not erased. The fairy folk, like leprechauns, are considered remnants of pagan gods that went underground as Christianity advanced. Indeed, the two share the characteristics of being capricious, unpredictable "beings" of the earth and natural forces.

Atop cliffs like these, the flavor of an earlier time can creep in by osmosis. More than anything else, Ireland is a place of spiritual reinvention—how can it be otherwise? The barrier between earthly preoccupations and greater mysteries feels very thin, and even one's corporeal being is lighter, unburdened from earthly concerns. The mood is suggestive—an unbounded field of sea and sky where anything is possible—then, in the seventh century, as well as now. On Dingle, I reveled in an ancient culture of my own imagining, one that was tolerant of serious inquiry, because that's what I grew up with. My problem is with the aftermath, when conclusions have been drawn, hierarchies of power have been constructed, and those anointed with spiritual authority, abundantly sure of themselves and their version of things, are not worthy of their posts, as so often happens. I don't like what religions become. I like what they *start out* to do before the original, illuminating ideas, myths, stories, poetry are muddied and corrupted. Before the moment ever happens when the exquisite thing that one simple person wrote or felt or tried to do is used in a bid for supremacy and control.

About twenty-three miles out to sea from where we stood was a spot that would seem treacherous to anyone but a seabird colony: a rock island called Skellig Michael. It comprises one of the most wild and remote sites of hermitage ever attempted. There, bony crags reach 218 meters skyward. Their steep sides are cut and laid with stone stairs that lead to six beehive huts, exactly like the ones on Dingle but much larger. They were built in the seventh century, along with two oratories. To go there and become a monk, a person underwent a sort of "civil death," not unlike a Buddhist retreat, severing all ties of affection and family. He lived with others who were strangers and would remain so, engaged in a "refinement of seeking," that they might be born again of Christ.[6] These pilgrims left the spiritual and societal establishment to recast themselves in much the same way that Deborah and Peter did.

There were numerous hermitages like Skellig Michael that split from the main branch and settled in other remote spots in Ireland. They then forged into Britain and Europe: Iona in Scotland (founded by Columba), Lindisfarne, Glastonbury, and St. Albans in England, and Bobbio in Northern Italy. That which was worldly and corrupt returned, for at least a while, to simplicity. Schools and new monasteries grew up around them; most are still in existence today.[7]

To me, it isn't too far a leap forward to the mid-twentieth century that my parents, alienated by the modern West and in flux about their own spiritual heritage, would have had similar reasons for coming here. The iconoclastic progress of Christianity through Ireland and beyond fascinated my mother. I remember entire afternoons spent hanging around ruins like these, with a picnic lunch in a verdant field, leaning up against ancient, sun-baked stones. My father, more interested in the geography and wildlife of the place, looked in his field guides or for fossils. My mother wandered about, looking and listening for a clue to a new direction, while I played with my trolls or watched the animals.

Although suffering from a persistent metaphysical alienation, my mother was never dulled by it or made numb. During the *Annaghkeen* summer, she was thirty-eight, old enough to be dissuaded, to settle for the intermittent providential gleam and let her own experience be shaped by external structures. She did try. I remember her taking me to St. Anne's, a one-story stucco church in our town on Long Island. She went every once in a while, as if compelled. Once seated in the hard wooden pew, she was brusque, as if she were having a checkup at the doctor. She'd sit there, trying to absorb the bitter elixir. She wrote:

I wish, I wish, I wish I could join up; all through the years trying to edge closer. In Europe I hung around churches as others do art galleries or bistros. I sneak off to church to take communion, to celebrate something, partake, hand myself over.

During the *Annaghkeen* summer, my mother was still on the path of reason—if only she went to the right place, had the right thoughts, strung together the right group of words, she could find a way to join, to hand herself over. As I've thought many times, it's hard to know completely what happened to her, and consequently what happened to me. What would I have been without the influence of her particular, uncommon spirit and its early end? Losing a parent early prevents one from ever fully adding or subtracting them from the equation because they no longer have a shape in the world. In a strange way, their shapelessness leaves one mutable, full of holes. I myself can't join up, but unlike my mother, I don't feel the loss. I would never be able to believe the answers. Though I'm a bit of a cynic, I'm full of respect for the questions and believe that the act of asking is its own form of prayer. For me, answers come in circuitous and unpredictable ways that are never fully fixed, no matter how much religious ideology attempts to classify them. As a child of Zen and a fair amount of loss, I can only say that I'm informed as much by what is missing as what is there.

Maybe that is why, looking out over the sea, I could feel the ghosts of the pioneering seers and seekers who came through this place, as well as my mother's spirit still. Dingle, indeed any barren coast in the southwest of Ireland, is a departure point— it has a feeling of being left over and over again. Achingly beautiful, abandoned and abandoning, instructive and careless. Sun, sea, rocks, seabirds, heather, and ferns. Not much to go on. In fact, nothing at all. Clouds, sky, a stretch of blue without limit . . . a simpler quest, a chance at pure, unadorned discovery.

Fallen Gods

Because he experienced it in childhood Innisfree still be-
longed to Yeats years later when on a London Street he heard
those low sounds in the deep heart's core. The child is pure sen-
sation, not yet lost to striving, and the scenery of his days is in
the tissues of his body.

In the morning at our new bed-and-breakfast, the first thing
Emmett wanted to do was to check on a note he had left
the night before for the leprechauns. He wondered if we had
left enough biscuits. I assured him that leprechauns, being
so small, are light eaters. They never dragged more than one
whole cookie away at Annaghkeen.

To my surprise, my six-year-old was skeptical. Unfortunately, he is forever among adults who are talking about what's
true and what isn't and has been persuaded that this is the most
important consideration. During the *Annaghkeen* summer, I
was a year older than him and never skeptical about fairies. I
knew that to try to impose empirical theory upon them was
a bad idea and no fun. So I told Emmett that doubting them
might insult them, and that insulted fairies could be wicked.
In the window box, we found the saucer empty but for a few
crumbs, and the note opened and tossed to the side.

Dear Leprechauns,

I would really really LOVE to see you, but I don't quite know what I want to do with you (just keep you as a pet?). If you are real, this would be a note for you. Don't appear anytime when I'm sleeping. I don't want you to do a trick on me, and no Pookas, because my Mom says they are scary.

I'll also leave some food for you. I don't want to show you to people on the plane, I just want my classmates to see you for show and tell. I don't know what will make you mad or what will make you happy and so if I make you mad, don't get mad at me. I also do want your pot of gold. By: Emmett

Since seizure and pots of gold seemed to be his point, I said that we would take the camera again and try to "capture" one on film. Today, we would be driving to Dingle town. Along the way we would photograph prime spots, like tree hollows, rock ledges, miniature streams, and moss meadows.

At breakfast we went over different types of fairies we might encounter. From Dermot MacManus's *The Middle Kingdom* and Yeats's *Irish Folk Stories and Fairy Tales*, we had learned that there were many. And the crux of fairy sightings is that they are best, and indeed only possible, in the deep countryside, where fortunately we found ourselves. A game of hide and seek is finest at twilight, or "betwixt the two lights," as MacManus wrote, ". . . as countrymen dig in the fields and bogs in the gentle summer evening and stroll home . . . as the girls milk the cows and with clever hands coax the last drops from the udder . . . so long will they be close to the powers that live and pulsate in nature; and in this country those powers are, above all, the Shee, or, as the English call them, the fairies."

The books were quite an elaboration on my scant experience, consisting only of leprechauns and their wives and tiny, delicate children with clothes of new maple leaves and hair like dandelion down, hiding out in the hollows of the monkey puzzle tree on the island.

We learned that the term *Shee* came from the Gaelic words *Sleigh Sidhe*. In this general category were leprechauns, clurichauns, banshees, far darrig, changelings, merrow (mermaids), and Emmett's dreaded pookas, described by Yeats as being "half in the world of form" and usually appearing as a horse or a donkey: ". . . on solitary mountains and among old ruins he lives, grown monstrous with much solitude, and is of the race of the nightmare . . ."

After the introduction of Christianity, pagan deities were demoted and took to living out of sight underneath the earth from whence they came. Though not, as any knowledgeable country person will attest, denuded of all their power.

We watched some American backpackers pile their plates high at the buffet, which was much the same at the Four Winds. They were at the next table, and so struck up a conversation with us. Like many people staying in Ireland in budget lodgings, they were here for only one night while backpacking their way over the whole peninsula. Like us, they were eating as much as they could. Our big discovery: every B and B has a kettle, and "Pot Noodle" (a sodium-riddled British product in a big plastic cup) costs only two euro. For dinner, we'd spread newspapers on the floor and cook it up, stirring in chunks of cheese from the breakfast buffet. Yesterday, Emmett had had an expensive sandwich for lunch, and we did without.

I pushed some rolls across the tablecloth for Steve to put in his jacket pockets and secreted a banana and some small Gouda cheeses into my bag. We prodded Emmett to at least eat a little more toast while he had the chance. Sausages, more sausages, bacon, fried tomatoes and potatoes, eggs, white pudding, and the gamey, ubiquitous black pudding, which is really blood sausage. I washed it down with lots of the funny-tasting orange juice. One of the backpackers smiled and warned us about the blood pudding. "It gets to you after a while," she said, and I believed her.

There is a proliferation of traffic circles in Ireland now. Circles are inviting, inclusive shapes; they don't cut you off. Circles make a terrific combination with traffic—if you can't decide which of four turnoffs you want, you just keep going around and around until you figure it out. Roundabouts, as they are called here, pose no barriers to your quest. If you are lost, you don't get caught in traffic or at stops; you just keep whirling on and off various rotaries with the illusion of getting somewhere important. Thus it was with us. The Gaelic sign for Dingle town *was* confusing because it was in small letters under *An Daingean*, its Irish name. In some cases, the English name wasn't even on the sign. Later, I was reminded by my guidebook that all the signs in Kerry would be bilingual because we were now in a Gaeltacht.

We came into the town with the port on our left, a cheerful jumble of fishing boats off a long concrete pier. Midsized fishing trawlers with net draggers fanning along their flanks seemed the mark of authenticity for a real working town. In front of them perched "Fungie," a bronze statue of Dingle Harbor's resident bottle-nosed dolphin, worn shiny by many children's hands. Emmett was delighted with the boats, and so was I. Steve, who really loves a town, registered pleasure with a small upward curl at the corners of his mouth. And we had a chance at real coffee here.

We went walking, noses cocked to the wind for the scent of roasted beans, up the middle of the three main streets which inclined slightly from the bay. The little houses and pubs climbing up the hill had the accidental charm of British Isles architecture, where varying styles represent different purposes and undulating rooflines crowd together in a row as if to say, "I see things differently than you, but here we are." Further emphasizing the distinction was that each had its own Caribbean color: hot mustard here, deep purple there, cobalt blue, a cross between fuchsia and maroon, light pink, deep green—a new thing since I had last been here. It occurred to me then that we had not yet seen one of Ireland's iconic symbols: a thatched-roof cottage. In the sixties, many of the cottages dotting the countryside had had roofs made of long-stemmed wheat straw.

As we picked our way up the crowded street, I saw a group of children with milky, lightly freckled skin, hair the color of new rust, and sharp clear eyes that reminded me of a long-cherished picture of my babysitter at Annaghkeen, Philomena Fahy. She was fifteen. She is captured forever in a photograph my mother took with her Rolleiflex, seated next to rumpled me on the steps of what is probably the Mulloy farmhouse (next door to Annaghkeen). In the picture, Philomena is prim despite the white-lace slip showing just over her bow-tied, pointy-toed shoes. Her black hair is smoothly coiffed, her pressed shirt is printed with pastoral scenes, and she holds a ball of yarn from which I draw a thread onto knitting needles. It was hard to believe that she would now be fifty-six years old.

It was easy to pick out the natives. We saw a variety of the classic Irish coloring: black hair and blue or brown eyes, descended from the "original Irish," the Milesians of the Iberian Peninsula, and the tall red, blonde, or brown-haired, blue-eyed, freckled combination that descended from later invaders—the Gaelic Celts and Vikings. Many town-goers were dressed semi-formally, in pressed skirts and slacks; in America they would be on their way to a wedding or a funeral. Even the ancient men on the benches wore tweed sport jackets with corduroys and leather shoes.

Sharply dressed young businesspeople flowed around the old timers, and tourists did their slow, poking weave: Americans in sneakers, shorts, and fanny packs; Germans in brightly colored hiking wear; a few well-shod Italians strolling and laughing, seemingly undisturbed by espresso deprivation.

Aside from the physical characteristics, there's a quality particular to most Irish—a general modesty, a refusal to take up space that is still in evidence even in the post-millennial world. When the women are pretty, it's as if they are spun from sugar. They aren't earthly creatures; they are fairylike, like Philomena. My mother wrote of her:

She is the Irish girl who waits in sunlight and shadow, who dances in the glen while the pipes are playing; curly hair and dark eyes, a straight short nose and truly, not roses, but peonies burst in her cheeks through whitest skin.

There were many Philomenas that day in Dingle. Also a few fine-looking fellows just in from the fields. In overalls and work boots at the hardware store, or on the threshold of a pub, they have the easy appeal of men who have spent most of the day outside.

My father said that Irish women "had no sex appeal," but my mother thought the Irish men sometimes very handsome. In *Annaghkeen*, she wrote about a farmer we met on the road as we were walking:

He had black eyes, bright like bits of glass. The eyes are the difference in the men and women of Ireland. Though the women are handsome, they have not the beauty of the men. That comes gleaming

from the eyes, a glance from another dimension playing about the
straight look of life.

My mother, aware of her own beauty but unable to inhabit
it as a consistent theme, missed that for the farmer *she* was the
transport to another dimension, and not from the modesty a
tolerable narrator must assume. She felt the same about all her
features and accomplishments; they were apart from herself.
She had no way of internalizing an event, a piece of luck, or a
compliment the way most people do, by putting it in a com-
memorative pile to themselves. It was a flaw, as well as her
distinction. Intelligence, talent, beauty, a published book, her
husband and children—all got a somewhat cocked expression,
like a bird at a nest site it finds unsatisfactory.

Like our town of Sag Harbor once was, Dingle is a fishing
port, and like most fishing towns, it is colonized with pubs,
many of which were in full swing on this Friday noon. The
variety was almost as great as the number: there were large,
modern pubs and pubs so small that five was a crowd; one that
sold Wellingtons and leather belts; another that sold sheets and
blankets; and another that was a hardware store too, selling everything from beds and bicycles to creosote and fertilizer.

Aside from the coffee situation, Steve seemed at home in
the entire country, as if he had belonged here all his life. His
forebears could easily have been domestics for the families
of either of my parents, who employed the Irish as nannies,
housekeepers, cooks, and gardeners. Steve's great-grandfa-
ther and -mother came to Boston from Ireland and England in
the late nineteenth century. I heard that the following generation had owned a few shops. His grandmother was the first
in her family to go to college. His father, Robert, was a music
professor for most of his career. When I asked his father about

his forebears in Ireland, he spoke only the name of one town: Portumna. The word Portumna dropped from his lips like a plum—all one needed to know. He visited Ireland once, didn't even go to Portumna, sticking to Dublin and the Ring of Kerry. The father of seven children, he was more interested in the future in the U.S., for himself and for his children. The past was the past, and it was best that it remain there.

Steve's paternal grandparents might have been from Portumna (not far from Annaghkeen) and might have gone to England to work before immigrating to the U.S., but that's the end of the information I could cobble together. O'Shaughnessy (the same as Shaughnessy) was among the most common Irish names of the great emigration. To find the original family would be a huge task. Steve didn't seem that keen on it. Unlike me, he doesn't see the use of connecting dots back through time. He prefers to remain in the here and now, like his father.

Steve's salaried job is teaching middle school orchestra, and in the busy season he plays in bookstores, musical productions, receptions—anywhere and everywhere, hauling one of two double basses or stacks of amplifiers up and down the stairs to and from his music room. He talks about the drama of getting paid after the gigs. The partygoers, wedding families, and bar owners are always trying to stiff him, and he has to wait around into the night sometimes to get a check. And then the bar owner or the father of the bride puts a ten-dollar tip into his hand and says to the band, "Split it up." It's a rough sort of male world that he's at home in. A world that is sized up in small amounts of cash. During the school year, the extra money slows to a trickle, and he teaches violin to kids at their houses until seven or eight at night, often charging according to what the parents can afford. His father, who also did many side jobs, used to say, "A little wool from a mangy sheep . . ."

which Steve repeats, and we laugh. It's the modesty of it that I love. Nothing is abstracted. He has a good job but never turns down extra work, as if there might be a sudden paucity of food or an apocalypse of some kind. He and all his family are very frugal—I think it might be the cultural legacy of famine, but he would argue with me. He goes out, makes these extra twenties, tens, and fives, and spends them at the grocery store on food and things for the house. I picture him, leaning over rows of frozen peas, thinking about what to put in the cart, thinking about some little extra thing we might like. It is all so incredibly abundant to him—nothing is taken for granted. A candle. Greek yogurt? Tangerines. He calls several times a day and asks, "How're you doing?" He's on the phone at home, arranging the gigs, reheating the food he gets from the new gourmet grocery store an hour's drive away. Unloading bags and bags of food from the supermarket. The kitchen freezer, the basement freezer, and the cupboards are bursting with food. We now have, stored away in the top cupboards, at least eight boxes of oatmeal and fifteen boxes of pasta in every size, shape, and color.

In contrast, my father rarely dealt directly with money, much less with groceries, but instead had agents, accountants, and wives. His relationship was closest to whatever he was writing at the time, and his family was always second to that. The public was at a remove as well, benefiting just from reading his books or being in the same room with him hearing him speak. When they met him, they were entranced by the dichotomies at play: patrician and liberal, icy and warm, remote and comforting, moth-eaten and elegant, boyish and masterful, in the room with you and one thousand miles away. He rigorously maintained the distance that he needed from anyone who needed something from him. Excepted from this were people who he believed had suffered, who were made honest and worthy by deprivation, whom he could help. Unfortunately, no matter what happened to his family, he saw us as sort of spoiled and had no respect for that, in the same way he hadn't any respect for himself, having been born with a silver spoon in his mouth.

My father walked away from his privileged beginnings through a kind of service that he did. This went much deeper than noblesse oblige. He was a tireless warrior for American Indian groups, Leonard Peltier, the migrant farm workers and their leaders, the local fishermen on Long Island grinding out a living under the restrictions the sport fishermen had imposed. He worked assiduously for the environment and the rights of people less lucky than himself, but his compassion did not extend to us, the people who had chosen to be with him or landed with him somehow—his family. The guilt that drove him extended to us, so we were guilty too. The only way to escape the guilt was to not be selfish, to save the world in order to save ourselves, or to just make ourselves palatable. My stepsister, Carey, was fond of saying that in his eyes you were no good unless you were "washing the foot of a leper." Like many of the funny things she said, that one had a particular biting truth to it.

Another notable preoccupation was the women. There were plenty: fans, acquaintances, friends, or students (sometimes Zen students). I don't remember once seeing him let a pretty girl go by without making some sort of comment, or taking a second look, or turning himself into a more animated conversational partner. It was a tic that only someone close to him could see; he flirted clandestinely. He knew how to manipulate people, making it seem a brilliant coincidence as they discovered that his wishes were really what *they* desired. He knew the power of his own image: the last patrician, politically almost impeccable, intellectual, solvent, the WASP bachelor—

no, wait, he only seemed like one—that reminded them of their fathers and their sexy science teachers and their sons all at the same time. They were mostly unaware that the puzzle of his opposing sides was completely irreconcilable. The women kept coming, all of his life, through all of his marriages, determined to possess him for themselves, to succeed where so many had failed. If they couldn't do that, they wanted their children to emulate him, and with glowing faces trotted their darlings up to meet him. He was what they aspired to, he was the Holy Grail, the "Ultimate Man," as his friend John Sherry joked. As he got stuck in something and unstuck again, he was barely able to count them or remember details—except for the general wash of a good time, he was left almost as clean as a whistle—because they weren't his idea, these women, and so each one, each time, produced in him what looked like genuine surprise. Don't ask me how I know about them all; he never spoke about them, and I never dared ask. They were just there—a backdrop to my whole life as a child, sending toxic plumes down the chimney, fingers of ice through the mail slot, tearing up the house all the time with their desperate desires. Over time, I came to feel, in a nonlogical sort of way, that these witchy multitudes were focused on vanquishing my mother, and that in the end they prevailed. I also felt that I could never be good enough, accomplished enough, or pretty enough to warrant much of his attention. In this, my father was complicit, not because he willed it, but because he overlooked it. He was always isolated in his work.

I think it was in Paris that my parents first got together. They had a running joke that perplexed me when I was growing up.

My mother would say, "Don't you remember, Peter, when we met in Paris at that party? Why can't you remember it?"

"You *think* you met me in Paris, but it must have been someone else. You've gotten it mixed up. Again."

"How could I have mixed you up with someone else?!" she'd say, laughing in a delighted sort of way.

Paris as the location of some sort of major happening between my mother and father was so ingrained in me that I may have conjured up events out of thin air. At *The Paris Review*'s fifty-fifth anniversary revel, where my father was being honored, Erik Satie's "Gymnopédie No. 1" was played. As the piece meandered and wound its way above the five hundred or so guests at their tables, I had an intensely romantic "memory" of Deborah and Peter in the fifties, which nearly brought me to tears. There was something so unfinished about it, and terribly sad. As the music played, I "felt" their love, I "saw" them by the Seine, at the Tuileries, coming out of Shakespeare and Company hand in hand—all of this as real as if I had been there. So blinded by emotion was I that I mistakenly shared this with my stepsister Carey (Luke's sister), sitting to my right.

"Rue!" she shouted at me. "Dad was married to *my mother* in Paris!"

Accchhh . . . I pulled up sharp, sputtering apologies to my sister. So true, so true, I mused, while wanting to dive under the table. Yes, he was married—to Patsy Southgate, the mother of Carey and Luke. My oversight was typical of the Medusa hairdo that our family had by that time become, though it might have been one of the all-time worst.

For a kid, unlocking parental mysteries is like unearthing building blocks for living, for or against. There are the things one takes up, there are the things parents say, and then there is the real stuff. My assumption about Paris hardened over the years because there was no one to counter it. At a certain point much later, when I was grown, I realized that my own being to a significant degree was based on a supposition, made about a joke, made about an evening in Paris approximately eight years before I was born. I had superimposed a score, "Gymnopédie No. 1." My mother and father are young and sleek, she in heels and a swing dress, maybe the raccoon fur, and he in a gray gabardine suit and a fresh haircut. The blue-black waters of the river pass soundlessly behind them. The music plays. It is a moment, a droplet, a silvered wave—a culture that begins the next stage of a family.

The memory—not mine, and maybe not even real—is my personal page in the domestic lore, one in a stack of pages. Everyone knew about Dad and had one way or another been affected—Patsy, Luke and Carey, Alex, my mother and my stepmother Maria, and her children Antonia and Sarah. My page might be the strangest, as I came along as part of the baggage of someone no longer there to tell her side. I was further removed because I had originated, however briefly, elsewhere.

Eleven years after Paris, my mother was married to him. (Did she know he was living in the area she'd moved to? Had she planned it?) Then another five years went by . . . I was old enough to hear the few exchanged lines, always the same; I noticed the teasing eye over a five o'clock drink, a peanut popped into a mouth, a playful swat of a sentence: *You've gotten that mixed up. Again.* A mystery, a caress, a ruffle on the surface of deep waters, a powerful memory that wasn't mine yet made an imprint I will never lose.

After my misstep with Carey at *The Paris Review* party, I got up the nerve to try and parse out what was fact and what was fiction. It came to me all in a moment after a glass of wine over at my father's house. *So, why the joke about that party and Paris?* First, he was shocked that I remembered it, but then he was often shocked at the things I remembered. Then he coolly gave me his version. There was a *Paris Review* party, hosted by some women from the Sorbonne, one of whom was my mother. That was it. When I asked what was so funny about that, I got an icy blank stare. He said that they didn't meet again until years later, on Long Island. My mother was on the beach, wearing a black bikini—and she was wearing it very well, he added. It was then that they started "going around together," he said. It was absurd for me to have expected something other than varnish on the Paris story, but I hungered for a few patches of light upon a past so tangled up and lost.

To be absolutely fair, I can't imagine what details he could have gone into that wouldn't have made me uncomfortable. The confusion comes from the indelible nature of childhood, the things that happen, the details and images that replay over and over and turn us, for better or worse, into the people we become. Maybe this is why people make such a romantic boondoggle of children and their own childhoods. My mother did; I do. We can't choose, we're nailed to it. The terrain is laid down before we're born.

In Dingle, we found ourselves back at the docks, the afternoon light glinting across collapsed nets and rusty chains. We strolled along Strand Street, where the tourist shops were bedecked in tacky green and tartan, mugs and shot glasses with maps of Ireland printed on them, and all manner of junk emblazoned with Ireland's most visible export—a vile, heel-clicking, pointy-eared leprechaun. Emmett dragged us into a shop, where we found a little boy speaking in rapid-fire French, trying to get his parents to buy him a beer mug emblazoned with the hideous green elves. Emmett was fascinated at the sound of him. The boy's mother smiled and shook her head, trying to pry the mug from his hands. I smiled at her as if to say that we didn't want to buy any of the stuff either. Then, with that silent understanding that parents of only children have, we got the kids out of the shop together and went across the street to a small grass commons next to the embankment.

The children found a dock hitch to inspect while chattering away, not seeming to mind that they were speaking different languages. I thought of a few people I knew at home who thought it was a waste, even destructive, to take a six-year-old overseas. "Shouldn't he be home in the life that he knows?" they asked. They were also concerned that Emmett wouldn't be able to remember anything. "He'll forget it all," I was told numerous times. I wondered what sort of forgetting and remembering they were talking about—there were so many kinds. I questioned why "the life he knows" was so highly rated that he should never want to leave it. Besides believing that children do get a lot out of travel, I wanted him to be able to be comfortable in different places. And lastly, I wondered how they could be so certain of their own experiences as children, which was of course what they were talking about.

Emmett, as usual, was as easily redirected as a toy boat in a bathtub. The boy, Thierry, had some marbles and plastic soldiers which he had laid out in the thick grass. He was sorting through which ones he would keep and which would be for their game, while Emmett got a solo battle going with the soldiers. Since the couple's English was as bad as our French, the conversation limped along. Knowing that they were staying at a hotel here in Dingle, we asked "Où est le café? Café? Café bon?" They were fit and good looking, and so unconcerned with the coffee situation that I thought they might be macrobiotic. We gazed at the children playing. I could feel us all inwardly having the same thought—that we were once just like they were. To the people who balked at our plans, I would say that the lovely absorbent quality of children doesn't last— it's mostly gone by the age of ten, which is all the more reason to take them when they are young.

The how or why of what becomes a memory is a mystery itself. My memories of the summer of 1965 aren't fit for postcards or picture books; they are more like three-dimensional pieces of time and place that I can enter as I would a room. Vivid grass greens, stones, cow pies, fossils in the walls, sloe-eyed cows, the mucky earth smell of the lake, my brother Luke joking with me and giving me rowing lessons, the farm next door, the animals, the mists and rains, the colors between my mother and father (frosty white, deep purple plum, chartreuse), the slow pace of things, the lack of parties and visitors and ringing phones, the comfort of having them almost to myself, as Luke was twelve and didn't need as much of their attention. Getting their attention simply because the house was small and I was there, and so were they, all day and all night. A few perfect nights in front of the fire, in the aftermath of some fight, everyone emotionally spent and talked out and exhausted enough to have given up and just accepted the others. Blissful moments, silent waiting moments, crystal clear "first" moments, waking up alone in a field, looking out over a gray lake, always inside an odd, skeletal, half-on-fire construction that I came from, that bore me forward, and from which I was already trying to get away.

The proof of a memory that people so desire sometimes comes in the form of a photograph. Light strikes a plastic material coated with an emulsion of silver halide crystals, changing them from white to black metallic silver. A projector shines another light at another time, projecting the image onto paper. Or now, images can be captured digitally and beamed anywhere one wants. It is truly magical. We pore over them, compelled by a linear hardness that never appears in nature. We are awe-struck at the captured moment, how we were different and how we have changed. We construct myths around photographs; they seem to be markers in time. They are evidence, objects we point to, to know ourselves.

Yet they can be so unreliable. I remember going over family albums with my stepmother Maria in the nineties. There were a few of Carey and Luke as little children being bathed in the up-stairs sink of my father's house. I said, "Oh yes, I remember it!" Maria looked at me incredulously, "How could you have? You weren't even born!" I had seen the pictures so many times they took up residence in my mind as a place I *was*. There are other types of embellishments. Out of the many family photos my mother left me, some are glamorous and Fellini-esque, elicit-ing sighs from my friends, but they don't represent the life that I cherished or a life that was even real. They are a few seconds of magic under the eye of a camera. The two I love the most are a portrait of my mother and me on a swing, and a brownie snap-shot of her laughing at a party in her college days in Colorado.

Children aren't interested in looking at photographs. Ex-terior representations are not relevant to them because they have so much more going on. Most hate being photographed, making faces from the moment they understand the process, effectively ruining it. They are naturally contemptuous of our attempt to forge separateness out of their only power—being in their lives instead of outside them. The very process of be-ing photographed takes them from where they *are* to where the adults are, outside looking in. They see the difference, the absurdity of the ritual—they sense that one day they will be as pathetic and stick out their tongues in an effort to make us go away. While we are trying to make the most of our precious time (struggling with camera settings and postcards and now jpegs we can post by email or on the internet, as if disseminating the moment to as many people as possible will make us remember it), they are weaving the surroundings around them like a chrysalis, to emerge later with a place incorporated into the self. My mother wrote this about me, in the foothills of the Slieve League:

Rue ran ahead, her feet circling faster and faster in the descending momentum. I see her still, so clearly, though why this "picture" I do not know . . . Certain casual moments have the clarity of shocking moments when, for an instant, the self is emptied and perception is not separate from belief.

That might be the essence of what we try to capture in pictures—the memory that pops up at odd times unscripted. I could have wished to have the same "picture" of Emmett and his friend on the strip of grass, though never could I have made the choice.

The sun came slanting lower now across the wind-ruffled surface of Dingle Bay, the boats, and the playing children. We collected them and walked farther down Strand Street, where another row of shops belched their wares upon the sidewalk. There were racks of leprechaun beer mugs, T-shirts about beer and beer drinking, and infant wear with "Baby Mic" stitched across the front. I was personally embarrassed in front of our French pals because the place reminded me of Times Square. Everywhere, monstrous elves danced on postcards and T-shirts, hoisted back pints of beer while stuck between breasts with four-leaf-clover pasties, their pseudo-wicked grins aflame. "Have a Fookin' Brilliant Day," and "Kiss my Shamrock," and

"Want to Play with me Leprechaun?" were but a few of the exhortations from these, the most recognizable of the fabled fairy folk. The kids pulled us around, and we reluctantly followed. I picked up a set of coasters that read, "Dance as if no one were watching, sing as if no one were listening, and live every day as if it were your last." I thought it excellent advice, though if my last day were to be in this shop, the joke would be on me.

The Celts, the missionaries, the Vikings, the Anglo-Normans—Ireland's past is strewn with invasions. Though heavily influenced by the interlopers, the Irish kept their own counsel, in part through folklore that was handed down over centuries. As I strolled around, it occurred to me that despite the vulgar T-shirts, the fairy folk are an ancient *collective* memory, which is not that different from a personal one. Both protect the inner life; both *are* the inner life. Both surface in times of extreme emotion or in tranquil places such as the deep countryside.

I rifled through bins of tacky posters, four-leaf-clover lanyards, and Guinness memorabilia. One T-shirt leprechaun was an erect penis with a red hat and green coat and a black-ringed leer pasted on. I tried to conjure the faces of the revelers as they picked these things from the shelves to take home for their wild night out. The company retreat, the gangs of students, the packs of "yobs" on a Saturday night. Drunkenness and abandon are only other ways to refuse the material realm and refer obsessively and exclusively to one's particular set of memories.

The last T-shirt in the row said, "Get Lucky with a Leprechaun," which made me think how Emmett had already, and how much I had as a child, though in a different way than the T-shirt writer intended.

My mother and I went leprechaun hunting everywhere: on the grounds of Ashford Castle, around Annaghkeen, and in all the places we traveled to that summer. Together, we left out cups of milk and biscuits and wrote long letters which were miraculously gone in the early morning while the mist still hung over the lake. Under the tall pines and the strange monkey puzzle tree, around each bend of what seemed like such a big place, next to the two garbage heaps along the house—named (by the owners) Cloaca Maxima and Cloaca Minor—one might luck upon a flurry of tiny hands and feet and faces scurrying for cover, or perhaps pushing off from the retaining wall in a wax paper boat, faces smudged with pine bark fires. I spent entire days peeking under bushes and behind rocks and trees, the drama of a sighting ever present in my mind. Their clothes would be made of discarded dishtowels, their mattresses from woven pine needles, their green hats from bits of discarded felt from one of my sewing projects with Philomena.

Once, I found this letter addressed to me, propped up under the pine trees next to an empty shot glass of milk:

Dear Child,

Thank you for the blankets and the milk. It was so kind of you to think of us. Not many people do anymore.

Forgive our handwriting. It takes three of us to push the pen which we found with the paper in your kitchen. We also took a cookie for a sweet to follow our mid-night feast.

Oh, lovely child, come back to Ireland. We have watched you for a long time, followed you through the lanes of Ashford, in the forest of Inchagoill, on the cairn of Annaghkeen, and we shall miss your dear presence.

Farewell—we bless you for you believe—

Deirdre, Maura, Pegeen—chief firelighters to the Queen and the Queen herself, Maeve. Sean, 'Seamus, Shane and Strongbow the King—the first three being his chief firelighters.

I read it over and over, and took it everywhere with me on our travels through the countryside as proof that the little people really did exist—and no one dared argue. Later, I was able to understand more about the stories and what she was trying to show me. As the collective psyche of Ireland had survived, so we too would survive by cultivating a strength and power that was hidden—a magical, labyrinthine web underneath a delicate, always changing surface.

The T-shirt scribes were right about one thing: residents of the fairy world keep their own merry society among mortals, partying most of the time. Denizens of the underground, they love to mimic and confound the humans in the world above. They are jealous of the mortal realm. Some say they were once angels that fell from heaven, but not so far as to descend to hell. So they are forever poised at a frustrated midpoint, nursing their obsessions, mimicking the humans and playing pranks because humans *might* get to heaven, but they won't, ever. Unlike the all-knowing God that took their place, in the fairy stories, high ideals don't play much of a part; wisdom is gained through fate and experience. The grown-up in me thinks that rings true.

Yeats wrote: "Many poets, and all mystic and occult writers, in all ages and countries, have declared that behind the visible are chains on chains of conscious beings, who are not of heaven but of the earth, who have no inherent form but change according to their whim, or the mind that sees them. You cannot lift your hand without influencing and being influenced by hoards. The visible world is merely their skin. In dreams we go amongst them, and play with them, and combat with them."[8]

The fairies are just symbols for every absurd and strange duality as seen through one's own lens—often not matching up to anyone else's—and yes, swayed by forces beyond one's immediate understanding. Have I encountered the fairy folk in my dreams? Indeed, I'm sure I have.

I've always told Emmett (for he is a imaginative child) that to some people the imaginary realm is as real as the ground they walk on. It seems to me that a lot of odd, inexplicable things happen as we go about in the little bubbles in our heads. What about those rings I took off for a minute while lying on a green lawn that disappeared forever? What about the dream I had of a woman standing at the foot of my bed at two a.m., trying to get my attention, and then the call the next morning that brought the news that my grandmother had died? What about the way a lover perceived me decades ago that had nothing whatever to do with who I am? And I fell in love with him too, a chimera, a ghost, a blank canvas upon which I had sketched. With whom was I communing? What about the conversation that was interrupted by my mother's death? A conversation that seems halted mid-sentence to me to this day. What about the books she never wrote? The books that died with her?

What about any life that is extinguished yet accessible somehow, stowed away in the terrain of the still-living, a brilliant cut stone now and then unearthed, throwing off color and light against an expanse of sand? A holographic memory that is, inexplicably, *only* a memory. What about the way one can remember the past of an intimate friend even if that friend has never told us about their past? Or the way elephants conduct elaborate memorials for their dead, caressing the bones and mourning with sounds specific to the occasion? Despite millennia of scientific application, the constitution of the natural world remains enigmatic. In answer and interpretation, most people feel, in their unguarded moments, that the empirical world is only a skin for another one—a faint outline in which we proceed. Perhaps the vivid impressions that we so crave are only instants where we perceive the whole.

Outside the shop, we bade the French family goodbye. Emmett and Thierry departed one another casually, Emmett with a little wave, feeling no pull, no nostalgia, no prophecy of a lifetime of separation from the afternoon's events. Awkwardly, we shook hands with the parents, wanting to mark the convergence of ourselves in Dingle as a perfect afternoon on vacation, a story to tell, a picture to behold, but it had gotten away from us for all of our wanting. Too much present in the act of creation, we lacked the completion of the children. I watched Emmett taking in the items in the shop windows, listening to the soft drone of Irish voices in doorways, while I found myself again looking and listening through him.

In Ireland in 1965, the books and toys that were packed for me quickly lost their luster, and it seemed like we were there for such a long, long time. So my range expanded. As a child, I embroidered stories everywhere. There are places I could never put a name to that I took with me like a book tucked under my arm. Did I write it? Did Ireland write it for me? A summer in a foreign country turned out to later hold a kind of poetry, a tapestry of impressions that still exists in the far reaches of my imagination.

Ghost House Walk

Though this practice of Americans is much criticized, I think there is great value in dashing through countries. To look on the run often leaves impressions more vivid than when the eye is permitted to cross and re-cross a landscape and the brain to comment on it.

Still, I would like to spend some days around Killarney with time to float down the lakes, watch the changing light on the mountains; breathe, smell, feel the softness, the dampness, the luxuriance, the excessiveness.

After four days, we left the high-flying vistas of Dingle behind for County Cork. Skipping the Iveragh and Beara Peninsulas, we stayed on the southwest coast almost the whole way, about seventy-five miles. The diversity of terrain between the two places gave us a sense of vertigo, of traveling many more times the distance with giant steps. In half a day, we went from deserted, wild Dingle with its rock-face cliffs and dancing, silvery grasses to the grottoes of Killarney, Glengarriff, and Bantry.

Nestled along Ireland's southwestern tip at sea level, these villages are perfectly placed to sip the warmth of the Atlantic's Gulf Stream. They are mild in winter and almost tropical in summer. Plant life, such as giant rhododendrons, a bamboo forest (thirty varieties at Glengarriff Park), and Paleozoic tree ferns thrive here, some that are not found anywhere else in the British Isles. In the absence of the seacoast wind, the air is still and dense, though not oppressive. Here, the imagination contracts yet is moved to a greater precision under the shelter of a giant sessile oak than under skies that have no end.

We found Leyton House, a B and B in the seaside town of Bantry, down a suburban street that ebbed and wound down to the flats of Bantry Bay. My heart sank a bit when I first saw it. It was a row house, small even by Irish standards, with a tiny car park in front. I've come to realize that the Irish asphalt over their gardens at the first opportunity. Maybe, after hundreds of years of mud and rain, the tidiness of asphalt appeals to them, or maybe the owners of this B and B didn't want to struggle for a parking space. Whatever the reason, I thought it a shame. The bumper of their car almost obstructed the front door as we clambered past with our giant suitcases.

Once we were inside, Brenda Harrington, the proprietress, gave us a warm welcome. Along the low-slung corridor, there was a dining room to the right, then a sort of den to the left. We were invited into a teeny sitting room with a television, a coffee table with stacks of games, and, in the hearth, a small fake fire, a throbbing light inside a plastic configuration of painted logs and flames that never moved. Emmett waved his hands around it, marveling that it had no heat. A vacationing couple from the Isle of Man, solid and big-boned, were folded into extreme angles on the diminutive sofa.

Brenda brought biscuits and tea. "You're all right," she said, the tone of which fell somewhere between a question and a statement, the "t" a soft whisper. She pointed out videos for Emmett and came back a while later with more tea and to give me the pamphlets and maps I had asked for. Breakfast was between seven and nine-thirty. Her husband would give us directions if needed. Our bags were up in room number six, on the second floor, top of the stairs and toward the front of the building. If there was anything special we "would be needing," we had only to ask. "You're all right," she said again, which is a sweet thing to hear when so far from home. "Céad Míle Fáilte" is the slogan of the Irish tourism board. It literally means "one hundred thousand welcomes" and certainly proved true at tiny Leyton house. She vanished from the doorway on her way back to the kitchen to continue, we could only surmise, to toil at making our lives more enjoyable and perfect.

I had planned that we would cover a lot of ground in Ireland, never staying any place more than four nights (and most just three) until we arrived in the area of Galway where Annaghkeen Castle was supposed to be. From the start, we hoped to get a feeling for the country by going as we found it. It was to our benefit that even traveling with a child, lodgings were so flexible. There were at least two bed-and-breakfasts in every town.

The first day, Steve wanted to go into Killarney town, so we doubled back a bit. He still would not deign to drink the weak dribble at the B and B's, so every day began with the search for the precious elixir. I'd given up convincing him to change to tea because the tea was dismal too. Even our lovely hostess at Leyton made tea from bags. In *Angela's Ashes*, they are always breaking out the Barry's and lighting up a Woodbine, and here I thought I was coming to the *land* of tea. Yet so far I hadn't been able to find loose tea even in a supermarket; it was all box after box of tea bags. I had really looked forward to Irish tea, the attention to detail a good cup requires: a pre-heated pot, the right amount of good but not necessarily premium tea, porcelain cups, and never, ever a mug. I guessed there would be some modernization, but the high regard that the Irish have for convenience has trumped all. I was served, morning after morning, these small metal pots with clumsy handles with tea bags floating inside like life preservers and tasting sort of like life preservers might taste if one wanted to brew them.

Which makes me of a mind that one search is as legitimate as the next. The Irish looked for convenience, my search was for the past that I had lost and my mother, and Steve's was for a hot brown liquid caffeine delivery system. Where this quest might take us remained a mystery until our map unfolded each day. Yesterday, we went to Tralee, a nice big town. After a little drive around, we found an old three-star hotel just up the street with a big, very serious, gold and gleaming Italian espresso machine. The Hotel Imperial, it was called. Yes, yes, yes. Judging from Steve's face when his lips had left the edge of the small cup, we had hit the jackpot.

The next day, on our way to Killarney town, the traffic jammed up, as there was a soccer match. I wanted to turn back. As we got farther in, it began to rain. It wasn't just cars clogging the streets but lots of people too. Families in damp orange and red soccer shirts clogged the roadways, crossing to and fro from the gas station markets.

Dense mist collected on the windshield in fat rivulets. It was like sitting inside a cloud. Cars that had been backed up came to a complete halt. I was no longer sure we were even pointed toward Killarney—now beginning to assume mythic status as a coffee source. Steve was insistent, just go, go, *go*, he said, straight ahead. "Just push through," he kept saying, his finger pointed into the mass of traffic, while I wondered: Suppose we're pushing through in the wrong direction? Then I realized that because I was doing all the driving, we didn't need to agree. I swung into a mini-mall parking lot. A nice, helpful girl in a sweater store told me what all the fuss was about; the local soccer team was playing the Tralee team. Steve stalked off, while she added that getting to the center of town would take a long time today. She recommended "Muckross," a few miles from where we were. She said it was "a pretty place, with lots to do." Her enthusiasm gave me faith. So off we went, creeping slowly through the crowd of people carrying banners and singing soccer songs, Steve clutching his Styrofoam cup of pond water, and Emmett reading picture books in the back. After a few turns, the soccer crowds dispersed, and soon we were flying down a lovely road with huge old shade trees evenly spaced along a high stone wall. An unmarked opening in the wall was coming up, and Steve said, this is it, turn here. Sometimes he just gets a feeling. I obeyed, turning in between two high stone columns that seemed to guard the place zealously.

At the time, though we had my mother's book with us, we didn't know that we were at an *Annaghkeen* spot. The first part of the trip was meant to be an evocative meander; I had saved the specific destinations that I'd found in *Annaghkeen* for the end, as they were mostly concentrated around the castle and the island. That the girl in the sweater store mentioned Muckross was lucky, and that Steve had motioned us off the road was a bit more luck because later, back at Leyton House, I found that I'd been there with my mother, my father, and Luke. After we had crossed the Atlantic on the *Sylvania*, we had had ten days of sightseeing in the southwest before meeting Don and Carol Braider at the island. I didn't remember the name but had a general impression of my mother's chapter about a driver with hair the color of "turning leaves," a horse named Phil, and a carriage ride through a lovely wood.

Behind the wet stone columns, there were a number of drivers hawking rides, all approaching us at once. Patrick, an earth-toned fellow of indeterminate age, got there first. He said that a ride to the house, as well as a tour around the grounds and lake, would be thirty euro. Thirty euro was almost half our budget for the day. He might've seen our faces fall or taken into account our American accents and felt sorry for us. In any event, he dropped his price by a third. We were introduced to Max, a chestnut with a white blaze and white socks who rattled his tack in the drizzle. Up in the sweet wooden trap, there were two worn wool lap blankets that smelled of horse. With Emmett in the middle, we held a plastic poncho above our heads to make a roof against the rain. With Max at a sluggish clip clop—clip clop, we embarked upon a wide gravel path, Patrick flicking the long reins over his flanks to keep him at a good pace. Oyster-colored clouds clustered over the sun and across the sky, opening here and there to a promising stretch of blue.

Presently, we plunged into a deep wood, the path narrowing, the rain lightening as it was caught in the canopy. Scattered on either side among jadeite greens were the purple and pink azaleas that grew in such abundance here. Young trees, ancient liverworts, and ferns and mosses—many of which also lived as epiphytes sprouting on tree trunks and branches—composed the thick ground cover. Patrick pointed out a tall tree with scarlet blossoms at the top that he said was the oldest rhododendron in the park. It was about eighteen feet tall, with curving black branches and leaves splayed out like green stars.

As we picked up the pace to a trot again, I noticed a low droning mumble from up ahead: ". . . of Killarney Park . . . last privately . . . an American . . . house . . . a fortune out of a gold

. . . California . . ." Patrick's monologue buzzed away upwind from us like a fat lazy bee. I interrupted to ask him to repeat things, which made him falter; he had recited his speech so many times, he couldn't tell where he was in it.

Eventually, the rain weakened to just an intermittent drip. Sunrays poked down through the canopy, spilling onto the forest floor in splotches, setting damp blooms afire. Through the trees, we could see the dark water of Muckross Lake. The oaks gave way to a clearing, then a straight wide path lined with cypress trees, at the end of which sat Muckross House. It was a big neo-Tudor pile, as these relics from the industrial age are sometimes termed. On a peninsula between Lough Leane and Muckross Lake, it was about the size of an American Mc-Mansion. However, unlike the standard McMansion, which by definition dominates and overwhelms a modest building lot, this house originally came with ten thousand acres.

I found in my brochure that it was last privately owned in the twenties and early thirties by an American gold baron, William Bourne, who gave the estate to his only child, Maude, as a wedding present when she married an Anglo Irishman, Arthur Vincent. The couple had two children and spent most of their time here. In 1929, while traveling to visit her parents in California, Maude died of pneumonia. After that, Vincent and the children were unable to stay. Consequently, the house and its ten thousand acres were given to Ireland in Maud's memory. Their donation in 1932, along with former lands of the Earl of Kenmare, became the twenty-six thousand acres of what is now Killarney Park.

The front entryway had a plethora of mounted trophies of animals hunted on these lands. They included an enormous rack of antlers from the now extinct Irish elk, found in a local bog. Also present, staring mutely from wooden plaques, were the heads of Irish red deer. The upland areas of Torc and Man-gerton Mountains are home to Ireland's last remaining herd of about seven hundred. There were once golden eagles here, now completely extinct in Ireland due to egg collecting, hunt-ing, and habitat loss. There is currently a program in progress to re-introduce white-tailed eagles to Ireland. The park's wide range of altitudes and stony mountain outcroppings are attrac-tive to birds of prey who like to build large stick nests, called aeries, on promontories and cliff sides. Peregrine falcons still nest on isolated mountain crags here, and the osprey stops on its way between Northern Africa and Scandinavia. There are a wide variety of visiting birds: Greenland white-fronted geese, swallows, swifts, and cuckoos, on their way northward from Africa in the summertime.

From the public rooms of the house, tall windows looked onto the greensward rolling down to the lakeshore, the sun-swept water, and the almost pyramidal shape of Torc Mountain. I imagined the last red deer in Ireland looking down at us from in between the trees. As we went from room to room, each filled with gilded furniture and Asian antiques, I couldn't help being carried away by the elegance and wildness of it all, surrounded by thousands of acres of pristine parkland. Steve commented that, if not the last owners, then the ones before had enjoyed this isolated splendor while one million Irish died in the great famine. He reminded me that that was only one of the multiple cruelties imposed by the English onto this country and that all these grand houses were artifacts of centuries of exploitation. He was, of course, correct.

My lens befogged by too many Merchant Ivory films, it struck me that this house was once a bulwark against so much wilderness as well as a symbol of largess. I suspended all knowl-edge of history and pictured the family living here through the colder winter months, fires blazing, servants baking up breads, stripping game, and whipping cream. I could feel that at one time the house had attempted happiness, and for me, that endeavor softened its history. They too had lost a mother, a wife, a daughter, yet she remained a presence here. Then the beauty of this place was broken and could not be fixed.

In the formal library, slim imprints of sun fell past heavy curtains and across a salmon-colored rug just short of the stacks. In an adjoining sitting room, there was a French harp painted a strange yellow which interested Steve very much. I thought about my father's house in Sagaponack, how laden with my mother's memory it was. It still is. She's there every time I visit, and it seems as though she always will be. Though her attitudes about home were not in the least sentimental, the Sagaponack house was the last she had. While I gazed at the marble fireplace and the oil paintings on the wall of the last inhabitants, I wondered if this was all home to anyone, an echo of those still living and those who went before. I wondered if by the end, her feelings about home had changed. I pictured her in the hospital, feeling nostalgic about the last time she woke up in her own house, in her own nightgown, in her own bed, the day stretching before her in which to struggle with the windows and make jokes, write, and meditate far away from doctors and nurses and all that they signified. But it didn't ring true. My mother, in her fiery, wild woman sort of way, might not have missed home at all, might not have seen it, in the midst of her ordeal, as the place in which she hoped to land after it was all over.

In Sagaponack, there was a haunted house that she and I explored many times when I was small. We'd cross Sagg Road and step into a tangled wood, overgrown rose bushes hooking onto our coats. Then farther in, a wooden house listed slightly to the side, its dusty windows staring, its shutters hanging at odd angles, the porch collapsed but navigable with her walking stick. Her step was buoyant as she jumped up onto it, and I followed. We'd stay for hours, poking around. It was as if this wreck, with the sagging porch and abandoned furniture in ghostly outline in the window frames, was where she really belonged. Not at home cooking, arranging flowers, or doing something else boring, but in a fallen, abandoned house full of muted stories.

To me, home was wherever she was, so I wasn't frightened. I felt the same. The house was where she belonged, so it was where I belonged too, poking at the vines that were pulling down the porch pillars, analyzing the mechanics of ruin, peering into broken windows and rooms empty but for a few pieces of moldering furniture. Before the ruins of Ireland, the house was the truth *she* sought, existing and flowing in the interstices of change instead of trying, in vain, to create an illusion of stasis that could never be supported.

Conversely, to me, things around us were fixed, as they almost always are for the young. We are walking figures in a familiar painting, my mother not necessarily older than me. Around us, the brush strokes of the painting are static, and nothing changes, nothing at all. We walk, but our feet never move. On the forest floor, the leaves are packed, dry ruffles of orange and yellow rest over layers that are pleasantly damp and decomposing. Delightfully musty smells issue from the broken door of the house, an earwig waggles from a chair, there's the crow of a rook, the *whumpf* of a stuck window slamming shut.

Our two selves were not the same size, but in the painting I think of her as an equal. She rarely dictated to me, or presented herself as knowing more, or what to do. On these walks, and all throughout the *Annaghkeen* summer, I had the sense that I was her only ally. We were on a path that it seemed she wouldn't have chosen, but at least we had each other. It never occurred to me that she *had* chosen, that she *was* responsible. I only felt her confusion. Along with the confusion came her particular sort of ruthlessness in the silent bargains she was making—sorting people and things—throwing one to the side and bringing another to the fore, deciding what was needed for survival and what could be spared. The two of us were always in tandem, trying to untangle things, often without success, picking our way through a dark wood or a castle ruin like Annaghkeen—my mother dredging into the past, back to the beginnings, thinking, writing, and me believing that the past was where everyone had to start.

As I admired the sweep of lawn from the house to the lake, I could almost feel her disdain and see her face fall into the slackness of boredom. How pedestrian, she was thinking, how uninteresting. Later, reading *Annaghkeen*, I confirmed it—it wasn't this trumped-up confection of a house that had caught her imagination. It was, of course, the ruin of Muckross Abbey.

Patrick had given us only twenty minutes to wander, and we were almost out of time. We came out into shifting sun, while Emmett ran down the sloping green to the shore and up again, stopping to stare at the water now and then. Our circle widened, away from the formal gardens to the wide-cut lawn and the arboretum next to it. Patrick had told us that Muckross employs seventy-five full-time gardeners, and it was no wonder, I thought, looking around. The luxuriant and still air and the surrounding woods are like a cove in the crook of the peninsula, rarely getting any frost, bathed almost daily in light showers. In another clearing, we found specimen azaleas and rhododendrons dotting a rolling, green expanse. Emmett found one rhododendron the size of a van to play in; with pushed-back leaves for a door, he disappeared inside.

Some of the big Monterey cypresses and pines were planted when the house was built, and some are much older. Muckross has a number of common limes, cypresses, beeches, and alders listed in Kerry's tree register for their girth and height. One cypress in particular is at the top of the list. It is thirty-two feet wide and seventy feet tall. Steve said that trees throughout the British Isles grow so old and big because they don't have powerful storms like we do, especially hurricanes. As we wandered through the cooling afternoon, I thought that if there is another life, I would like to come back as a dogwood sapling, right on the edge of what is called the Camillan wood. Or maybe I could be that five-hundred-year-old yew, its great thick trunk rooted in an emerald carpet.

The older trees are out of a storybook, each tended regularly, season after season, with skills handed down through generations. Though they can look wise, they are also facetious, with the silliness of beings that have always been cared for. Their trunks are solid, but their branches reach for the sky with irrational curvatures, their shapes taut between the anarchy of nature and discipline. You know it when you see them; you know they are not normal. The foliage of one willow, cut straight across in a heavy, sweeping skirt, flows like a Valentino gown. A sessile oak, twenty-five feet across at its creeping, multi-fingered base, is a triad at its middle, one trunk-sized limb almost parallel to the ground, its crotch big enough to seat a family of four. All the attention has made them a mutation, older than they should be, with eccentric, heavy limbs and frivolous temperaments. They are strange jewels, a genetic outcropping, like supermodels and basketball players in an airport, traveling high above everyone else, an implied intelligence in their massive forms.

Though the rain had stopped, clouds were moving through the sky, casting mottled shadows over the wide green lawn, down the lakeshore, and over the indigo expanse of water, especially deep where the shadows raced. I had *Annaghkeen* with me that day in my bag, though I hadn't yet made the connection. Patrick had mentioned an abbey on the grounds, an ancient friary, but he said that it was closed for restoration. Steve, who is always interested in religious places, looked disappointed. So I pressed Patrick to take us there. Little did I know that ahead of us was the spot that my mother had written about the most.

We got into the trap and traversed the wood again, emerging this time into an open field. Just ahead, a bumpy stone structure sat against the forest wall, obscured in a metal cage. From the trap, we were able to see the roofless wall of the nave, and through the scaffolding, a large gothic window and seven narrow "lancet" windows along the side. As we came to a halt, Patrick said that there was a yew tree in the center of the cloister that had probably been planted more than 550 years ago. I was to later read:

A magnificent yew tree, said to have been planted by the friars at the founding of the Abbey, soars out of the damp cloistered inner court, and one can ascend to its height by climbing the stone stairs rising from the angles of the ambulatory . . . Yews have been found that are older than the ancient churches they stand beside, and perhaps they served as a canopied pulpit from which Druids spoke to an ancient crowd.

I fingered the spine of my book, where the silver lettering in cursive "Deborah Love" had begun to wear away. Muckross Abbey was exerting a pull that could not be denied. I asked Patrick if we could just poke around the outside and maybe glimpse the yew through the lancet windows. He looked both ways and said, okay, quickly.

We made our way through the tall grasses, the scaffolding looking taller, glinting in the sun, a metal cage over the graceful window and Romanesque arches. Underneath, the ivy had crept higher, generations of small animals and birds had come and gone, parents and children and grandchildren had walked through and departed, taking their memories home with them. Forty-one years were nothing to this place, while it had held onto my mother, and she to it.

A cloister is one of the happiest of architectural designs, for it realized so well the human sense of well-being; exposed, yet protected, snug yet exalted. An arching roof pulls one toward grandness, yet comforts with its shelter; air and light from the world come through the graceful arches looking onto the open court; the passageway is a direction, aimed, toward no end. It turns a corner, and another, and another.

To my mother, this abbey was all good things at once. There's no cost or commitment to anything except the repetition of rituals, performed anew every day with childlike innocence. In her imagining:

There is a stone reader's desk under the window lights and the monks listen to the psalm read by a brother. The psalm ends and silence again. The monks cross themselves and leave the hall; each to his task, or meditation.

The shelter of the cloister is *snug yet exalted.* The *arching roof pulls one toward grandness,* not an all-powerful figure that one is compelled to fear and follow. What and where is the grandness, the divinity? It isn't dictated, it's received by the *graceful arches* that let in *air and light from the world*. The building is a conduit to something organic and instructive, not authoritarian.

She then elaborates upon her sense of the retreated life here, the life that she wants, perhaps without even knowing it yet:

Concentration is devotion. Let him mend his habit, or read his psalter, cultivate the field, or stand beneath the fir trees listening to the wind. Nothing interrupts, except perhaps the inner voice of dread, reordering the world with words; to still it or leave it is his work and discipline.

To still the inner voice is one of the first tenets of Zen meditation. The perception/illusion of separateness and self, also called ego, is created by a governing conscious voice (*I am this, and they are that; it is this, it is that*). By silencing that voice and erasing the ego, one can begin to understand the nature of things, the universe, and oneself. In Ireland, my mother had not yet gone full bore into Zen, but all of her thoughts were leading her that way. We squinched our faces into the narrow windows, finding various sightlines, but none all the way to the center. First the scaffolding, then the three chambers—the refectory, the prior's house, and the nave. My mother's yew was sequestered inside a shell of steel and stone. Planted sometime in the 1400s, this tree had survived the dissolution of the monasteries by Henry VIII and the building's restoration by Franciscan friars who returned in 1626. It had survived even Cromwell, who razed the place by fire in 1652, forcing the friars to finally flee.

Once we were back at the trap, Patrick moved us a few paces back. He pointed out the yew and indeed, its pinnacled, prickly top was visible above the cloister. Equipoised with 550 years of birth, rebirth, and devastation, I felt (more than understood) what my mother had been trying to say. In the shadow of the eventual dust that she feels so keenly, she contends with having to make choices and assign importance to events or people, and then the "intelligence" of a flower occurs to her . . .

The flower hasn't this burden. The flower fulfills its immanence, intelligence implicit in its unfolding.

There is a discipline.

The flower grows without mistakes.

A man must grow himself, until he understands the intelligence of the flower.

As the tree oversaw the gyrations of history; as the flower naturally fulfills its immanence—the answers were inherent, lying within. Her thoughts just needed a place to converge, to come together in one pure and free-flowing direction. It must be free of dogma. It must be something intrinsic to her, which she would need only to realize.

When we returned from Ireland in 1965, she began looking in earnest. I remember her drinking hot chocolate late into the night, her desk covered with marked-up books, her typewriter clacking happily, her thoughts deeply absorbed in the effort to articulate what she felt. If only she could think hard enough, write clearly enough, she could abolish the obstacles between herself and God.

Idols shattered set you free. England for me is gone along with fathers, heroes, wise men, bank presidents and kings. This, an exhilarating and cruel time of transition while a generation wrests a new world from the old . . .

England was parliament and order—a romantic and patriarchal construct that had drawn my mother in as a young person. Ireland was wayward and independent, subjugated by England but not conquered, which was eventually much more interesting to her. Ireland's historic *oppression* resonated with her, the idea of closely held, secret beliefs and personal integrity separated from centers of power, be they the monasteries of the ninth century or the English for eight hundred years.

. . . for the secrets can't be kept in a world connected . . . the secret that the shaman knows no more than the tribesman; the man knows no more than the woman, the priest than the parishioner, or the parent the child.

Who will take their place? We will sit in rooms alone until we know.

The last sentence is a thumbnail of Zen practice which consists, mainly, of sitting meditation. Zen *sesshins*, rigorous two- to seven-day retreats, begin before daybreak with meditation, then chores, breakfast, meditation, and study all day. In these long periods (and shorter ones too), followers pursue *kenshō*, or an "opening" where the barrier between the self and the universe dissolve for a while, or even just one moment.

My father has often said that once my mother discovered Zen, she became almost completely absorbed in it, and it's true—it came through our house like a whirlwind. He might have been trying to explain why she was suddenly much more absent. It began with the lectures of writer and philosopher Alan Watts. Then she moved on to the Zen classics: *Zen Mind, Beginner's Mind*, *Moon in a Dewdrop*, and *The Blue Cliff Record*. She found the new Zen Studies Society on East Sixty-Seventh Street in Manhattan, a two-hour trip away from our house. Not long after, she went on her first sesshin. She received her dharma name, "Hoko." Weekend sesshins became weeklong sesshins, my mother away from us more and more. Sesshins require uniformity among Zen students to aid in the relinquishment of ego. A vegetarian diet, loose black clothes, and for the advanced monk a shaved head (my mother never got to this point, but I'm sure she would have). Along with meditation, students focus on the maintenance of the retreat: scrubbing floors and sinks and dishes, cleaning toilets, peeling potatoes, baking bread, weeding and gardening in silent worship—things that my mother would otherwise never do. The irony of having to leave home in order to do these simple, homey things is inescapable to me.

On sesshin, if the *rōshi* thinks you are not concentrated enough, they will whack you on the shoulders with the *keisaku* stick. But there's already pain enough built in. *Zazen* is long periods of sitting on a black round pillow, in silence, staring at a white wall, eyes cast at about forty-five degrees, hands cupped with two thumbs touching, fighting against the agony of sitting for so long in the "lotus" position, and fighting the mind's incessant inclination to think. After a number of these sesshins, or sometimes only one, students usually experience a great lightening and exaltation, as the burden of the self and ego have been lifted. The goal (though to *have* goals takes one out of the present moment and is not Zen) is to have a total opening, or enlightenment.

I have an insight into my mother's kenshō experiences, what they were like. Since I didn't see her very much once Zen came into our lives, my source is a picture of her, one of my favorites. It was taken in 1969, a few years after she got involved with Zen, not long before she was diagnosed with cancer. Taken somewhere on sesshin, presumably after a few days of deep and silent meditation, she is transformed. She is now Hoko, a woman who wants to sit for hours and hours not thinking. Hoko is in a kneeling pose, wearing a loose-fitting dress. Her face is positively broken open with joy, the crescents of her beautiful eyes laughing with freedom, wholeness, and more than anything—relief. I can't help but be glad that she arrived at something in her life that brought her such joy.

It helps me to explain her departure from our messy, confusing, strife-ridden little world in Sagaponack: the school, battles over my homework, sweet Alex, still only four or five years old, my father absent in his work or another research trip, the miserable housekeepers, the farty dog, the vast interminable ocean down the road, the house set in the midst of acres and acres of potato fields, as lonely as Dorothy's house after the tornado had its way. Kenshō was as if a door opened into a light more warm and pure and clear than any she had ever seen. And so, beginning in the late sixties, little men with shining bald heads and long black robes, first calling her "Debbie-san" ("Hoko" would come later) came out to the house in Sagaponack. The smoky pine smell of Zen incense filled the upper floors, and soon my old room upstairs was done over into a zendo, with rice-paper and balsa-wood screens over the windows, tatami mats, and Buddha icons. When the monks first appeared, I had no idea of the momentousness of the occasion, of what it would finally mean for us. Eventually, I came to hate them, smiling at absolutely everything, bowing and bobbing like ducks in a bathtub, getting their hooks into my mother. They were taking her away from us, from me. Did they really believe they were going to deliver her to salvation?

Probably no more or less than any of the *fathers, heroes, wise men, bank presidents and kings*, lovers, husbands, or wise children who had shown her the way before.

LSD and Zen

We skate ever faster over the melting ice. Rules, principles, institutions, codes dissolve as awareness forces us to release our hold; and one day we will find ourselves below, in a buoyant bath of pure melting and unimaginable distinctions. We will have no names.

We ate our lunch while Rue played among the rocks in the sunlit water. I watched her. Unlike the fragment of myself that teaches myself, weaving myself whole again with strands of information, she is a complete creature.

A few months before we left for Shannon, I went with my father to a memorial service at St. Anne's in Bridgehampton for a friend of his. As usual when we went to a church, I noticed how confidently he sang all the hymns, knowing every cadence, every word. For him, they were second nature. I was touched by the quaintness of this. Before, I had only seen him as a Zen student, then a monk, then a rōshi. He had been an austere figure in black *koromo* (robe), white *tabi* (slippers), and *shukin* (belt), coming in from the zendo in the barn at his house, sometimes hoarse from the chanting. The singing in the church was uplifting and cheerful, this thing we could do together. It was something, as opposed to the nothingness of Zen. As I tried to catch on to the melodies, I saw that he had deep associations there, yet my associations were few. He was a child of a completely different context than me, and my mother had been too. The sound of my father singing about God, supposedly *another* father, cast him in a different light, unique and strange. It made him smaller, less authoritative, and more approachable since, ostensibly, we were both under the umbrella of this supreme force that was going to take care of everything. I saw that as a boy he might have, for moments, days, months, or even years, believed this unequivocally, that when he was young his heart might have for a time been given over to some sort of complete resolution.

And then there was my mother, many years before. She'd taken me to St. Anne's, seemingly against her own will. Her face set in a kind of fury, she'd bow her head in prayer, as if daring God to make his case. I remember kneeling down and standing up along with the congregation, and clasping my hands together, my breath held fast, so I wouldn't miss any imparted wisdom that might come down from the sky above the church. I loved the light coming through the stained glass, the singing, the coziness, the candles, studying the back of people's heads and wondering what they were thinking. As soon as the service was over, we'd scurry out of there, my mother irritated and weary, and me feeling pulled away. I'd always want to go back to that somber, Christmas-y place of rich reds and blues, hushed wishes and appeals, the baritones and sopranos, some out of tune, and the white-robed figure of mysterious power. I loved all the people in the church and that afterward there was a coffee hour and time to play in the garden. I'd think about it every time I passed the building.

It seems to me a novel idea to have grown up in America as my parents did, with its founding religion as their own. It seems old-fashioned and sweet that the ritual of going to church was so integral to my mother that she kept checking in, even after declaring herself unable to believe. Of course, custom dictated that she and my father both engage in the rituals of friends and family: christenings, weddings, memorials, funerals, even long after their faith was gone.

At two weeks into our road trip, the question of whether or not we would be able to find the castle and the island was looming close. For me it had also been enough time away to feel, without the general busyness of life at home, chunks of my past fall into pieces like calving glaciers. A ghost of myself was jogged loose, a girl around the age of ten with a serious demeanor—that's what people said about me. At that age I felt as if I was looking out from behind a wall, and no one could see me. It was lonely but highly preferable to revealing anything. My mother thought I was strong and wise; my father thought I was tough. They were both wrong. I was going numb from all the changes. My exterior was freezing, leaving my face as blank as a sheet of ice.

It's hard to deny a person their passion, no matter what the cost. And in my mother's case, I wouldn't ever have wanted to. It takes a long process of growing up to forgive one's parents the things they needed, or even understand the things they needed. Even today, for most women of ambition, the struggle between being mothers and fully realizing their potential is neverending. So one wants to be generous. However, *children* are not generous, and it's largely from a child's perspective that I remember her and that I write.

Admiring the force that I was, my mother very much wanted to give me my own head. To try and make me into her version of a person would have been an infringement upon my dignity, as well as taken up too much time. Whose time? Mine, I guess, though as a child I had plenty. Hers, certainly. So I wasn't raised a Buddhist, but it was introduced into the atmosphere of the house as I was growing up. Oddly, it was reflective of the emptiness already there, a constant sad echo. Zen was austere, devoid of magic. Zen was a pinpoint of focus in a chaotic, unforgiving universe. Zen was an empty black box in the even bigger empty black box of the massive dark sky around the house in Sagaponack on a deep winter's night.

People on the outside beheld the whole Zen process with great suspicion. The light came from within—how was that possible? The understanding, already there, had only to be accessed with self-discipline. Followers of Zen were allowed their flaws, bringing them deep into the *hara* (lower belly, focal point of meditation), with great long breaths, accepting all. To outsiders, it looked frightening and cultish, and indeed in those days it must have seemed very strange. Inside the zendos, it was understood that followers would carry on with their regular lives when not meditating, and in fact, they were encouraged to. At the Zen Studies Society, there was no master plan that I knew of, no group efforts to recruit people. In keeping with the minimalist surroundings and doctrine, it was sophisticated and low-key. Zen didn't mean to interfere or take over anyone. My mother, had she lived, would have been one of the exceptions, though it is hard to say where influence ends and personal choice begins.

A few years after the Ireland summer, sometime in 1968, along with the monkish quiet in the house came the sound of Zen chanting. To hear people do the archetypal Zen chants, *Maka Hannya Haramita Shingyo* (Heart Sutra) and *Daihishin Dharani* (Sutra of Great Compassion) among them, is to really understand Zen, if one takes the time to listen. Each Japanese word is said with an emphasis that rarely varies, and there is little tonal individuation between notes. The chants are drones, very unified sounding, no highs, no lows, except at the end when they trail off on a sliding downward note, which sounds like someone dying, or at least running out of air. It is supposed to symbolize the perishability of all life and energy in its endless variation; it *sounds* like one "thing" or entity dropping off, leading to another thing being picked up, or born, at the beginning of a different chant in a different place. I disliked it because it seemed to have no context—i.e., it was no fun. (Had I been a Japanese child in a Buddhist family, surely I would have been better acclimated, though I might never have thought it was fun.) As a child, it sounded to me like just another in a series of endings and departures, causing things to fall more into pieces than they already were.

By the time I was eleven, Zen had fully arrived—the straw smell of the tatami mats, the rice-paper screens, the minimalist altars, the people with flowing robes, their faces still and peaceful and contemplative. I was deeply affected by what they were experiencing. I saw them and heard them and felt them all around me. The concepts made a mark on me—the interchangeability of all forms of energy, and again, something I was fast becoming familiar with, the unceasing nature of change. We are a part of it, we will change, and that is right and true. Zen tells you to let go, to stop trying to affix yourself to one thing or idea or person. It tells you that if you drop all the thinking and the effort to construct yourself, you will find that you won't fall and you won't disappear. You will find, as many people do, that there is a whole universe to hold you up. It can feel like floating down a miraculous sort of stream. Many people, upon discovering it, cry and/or laugh and look like surprised and happy children, years of worry dropping from their faces.

Early on, when my mother was just dabbling in Japanese tea ceremony and reading Alan Watts, she got me started. She'd say, "I bet you can't stop thinking completely for three seconds." And she was right; it was very hard to do. In my early twenties, suffering from anxiety, I began "sitting" on my own, on a *zabuton* (pillow) borrowed from the zendo my father had carried on in the old horse barn on his property. I did it mainly because of my mother's early lessons. I took that early challenge and built on it, though rarely *at* a zendo because I am suspicious of religious hierarchies of any kind. Though I respect—and to a degree, rely upon—the basic principles of Zen, I find an over-whelming paradox in having to follow a particular person who is anointed as a spiritual expert, especially *in Zen*.

But during that time in my twenties, I sat twice a day for long periods. I discovered what the people at the Zen Studies Society had found, that Zen was a place to go to gain a deeper understanding, to "refresh my life," as my father put it in his book *Nine-Headed Dragon River*. I found tremendous relief in it. Gradually, I was able to "float without thoughts" for a good while, and the anxiety went along with them. For the first time in a long time, I walked lightly and with a feeling of deep sanctuary on the path that my mother had forged. It was new to me, and at the same time anciently hers. The respite from my troubles seemed to come directly from her, my father, the universe, and the practice itself, clearing thoughts and the construct of the self away. I was tremendously grateful. It put my ship right in the water when I had nowhere else to turn.

It was also a way to be close to my father when I was away in college or overseas. When I was married, the zendo was the obvious choice for the ceremony, in part because Steve had been a Zen student even before we met. One of my father's monks, Dorothy Friedman, officiated. We married there because there was no apparent alternative, and because it was the least dogmatic place that I could think of. The last of my reasons was the most innocuous: it was home.

We will have no names.

After the *Annaghkeen* summer, my mother was inspired to bring Zen to the everyday in as many forms as possible, so Zen was in practical application in Sagaponack, as much as it could be for children. Many of the psychologists, psychiatrists, and writers of the time centered around a new movement called Sensory Awareness, which Alan Watts had dubbed "The Living Zen." Charlotte Selver, Elsa Gindler, Erich Fromm, and Fritz Perls were among many who pioneered the (then) far-reaching idea that each moment was a new moment, and that it was ideal to experience time in the present, as children did. It was believed that adults had everything to learn from children, instead of the other way around. This "new wave" taught that conventional child-rearing practice destroys their integrity, their sense of naturalness and connectedness. It was one of many movements that were unified around the new concept of respecting the intrinsic wholeness of a person and defending them from the societal, religious, and sexual mores that would separate them from it.[9]

It began to be my mother's perception that almost every "mirror," including the sort of preconceptions people have about one another, was fatal to any kind of worthwhile interaction. That the self-image that one carries through life was forged in their early years by sets of exterior images that were foisted upon them and were false. By adulthood, the person has entirely lost who they really were to begin with. A simple example might be the way people talk down to children as if they were idiots, and baby talk, which my mother thought inane and forbade in the house. She thought that if our environment was purged of such preconceptions (images that we had of one another, the images that were imposed on us by the larger world) we'd all find out who we *really* were.

After Ireland, the house became a microcosm of experimentation. The Zen people (silent!), the Japanese-tea-ceremony people (so silent!), my parents fervently writing away in their respective studios (also silent!), the loud strains of Bartók winding around the cathedral ceiling of the empty master bedroom on freezing winter nights, my father gone, and so many friends carpooling into psychotherapy in the city that their cars were nicknamed "flying couches." The housekeepers and any visitors or relatives were all stopped dead if they dared to send a *googoo* or a *gaga* my brother Alex's way. My stepsister Carey, who lived with us for a year, remembered that everyone was also under strict orders to never repeat back anything Alex said to him. "I want my ball," answered with, "You want your ball?" was forbidden. The correct answer was, "Here is your ball," or, "I don't know where it is," to avoid the destructive imaging.

But to me, "You want your ball?" is a gesture of encouragement. It identifies just who and what "you, your" and "I, my" are and shows that there is a responsive relationship across what might seem to a child an enormous kitchen or living room or garden. It shows support for the effort that was made. "You want your ball?" said in the right tone implies that you, adorable creature, should *have* your ball. It *must be somewhere* and *I will help you find it* is the cheerful subtext. Maybe there is a fine line between inanity and reassurance. Maybe there is a lot of dumb repetition while we impose our ideas of who the "other" is upon a child—but maybe, having no real alternatives yet, they really want us to. A lot of what we do to be close *is* just silly. Steve and I have been extremely silly and have the videos to prove it.

Steve and Emmett and I had already been weeks on the road, and we were doing pretty well for a long trip, even cheerful compared with the original crew of 1965. The other day, I noticed that Steve—kind and generous, uncomfortable drawing too much attention to himself—is like a transplanted offshoot of Irish culture, and so are his parents. The Shaughnessys are religious and reserved, with the sort of gentility that refuses to waver from stated positions. I've often thought that if you wanted a good spy who wouldn't divulge secrets under torture, pick an Irishman or woman. As we have seen in the pubs here, even the way they dance is within a form. They hold themselves rigid; there's a style and there is no embellishment to that style, no flights of fancy—the form is paramount. Yet Steve also says the Irish are bloody-minded, passionate, and dangerous (especially when drinking, when all that stubborn restraint goes to pieces). According to him, a certain sort of upstanding Irish citizen with barely a fleck of pastry on their lapel or a skeleton in their closet is the last person one would want to meet in a dark alley. In an exterior sense, however, the form is what they are and what they choose—a rigid cage that holds them togeth-er—and one can see it in the clerk paying out the change at the supermarket, or the slow and stately dancing at the pub, and in how well-behaved the children are. There's a certain sacrificial beauty in it, a way that it makes a case for the conventional, for traveling along established lines. I find it both amazing and ironical that three months in Ireland would have done nothing to temper my parent's drive toward the ultimate explanation for everything, would not have at least nudged them into a more reposeful state. Instead, they left at the summer's end to foray into the wildest inner spaces a person can go.

From my tranquil perch in Kerry, the glaciers groaned and squealed, ice and rock spilling from their sides in waterfalls. By the late sixties, the drugs were powerful, the music was great, the astonishments were many. No one was really a grown-up, or even home most of the time, yet in our estranged way we were all united in a sort of wild wager for the future. For those of us who hadn't much of a past, it was hard to tell what it was we were betting on. From 1966 to 1969, the soundtrack was The Beatles' "A Day in the Life," while things sped up, going faster and faster and at the same time extraordinarily slow in spots, like the few seconds before a car crash. The escalating war, the police brutality, the hammering gunfire, Vietnam on TV every night—these outrages and the reaction to them were rivet-ing for us children. We were being indoctrinated on one side of a war, without knowing what we were fighting for. We were surrounded by a sort of nebulous passion—both inside and outside of the house—and it was as terrifying as it was compel-ling. My reaction was to do as I had been taught and be as still as a Zen monk amid all that was going on around me. I didn't know it at the time, but my hope was just to survive.

I remember seeing and feeling psychotropic drugs blossom in our house, then crack into the cultural structures of our social circles and our town. LSD was everywhere: in the drinks, at the parties, in the music, on album covers and posters. To be far out was a good thing. Having your mind blown did not mean insanity but liberation. You were much better off *far out* with your mind blown (though my parents never would have used those terms). Huge gaps were developing between, say, fifth grade and what was going on at home, the former seeming in a kind of rigor mortis by comparison. I began to see the people who weren't tripping regularly as stuck and square. I had a sense that my parents were doing something serious that I needed to defend, and that their world and the regular world were different—another way that things were falling into pieces. At a camp in Canada, during a campfire lecture that was all about the evils of LSD, I held back from explaining that LSD was harmless, that it was an amazing tool. I wrote my mother the next day that I hadn't talked, though I had really wanted to. She immediately wrote back that I had done the right thing, along with the best care package I had ever gotten, with new pajamas and socks, a stack of *Archie* comics, and five bags of Sugar Babies, my favorite candy.

After the experience at camp, I got smart enough to realize that never could I have explained to the "regular" people— those on the other side of a rapidly growing divide—that my parents weren't pleasure seeking, but rather were looking for happiness, which is different. Later on in college, I took LSD a few times a week for one whole spring. It opened up the way I saw my life, I thought. I still think that, though it wasn't a great time to be a kid, the sixties were an interesting time. Having also practiced Zen, I understood why so many LSD users, including my parents, eventually turned to Buddhism.

Rules, principles, institutions, codes dissolve as awareness forces us to release our hold . . .

Under the leveling influence of LSD, energy and matter seem to be distributed equally—dwellers in a house in the suburbs are not less strange than African villagers in a hut, or (to put it another way) the family in the suburbs is *as exotic* as the villagers. All is accepted, the force of the universe is palatable, pulsing through the senses. Strangeness and ordinariness lose their currency, systems of punishment and reward, heaven and hell are flattened and impossible. In a typical psychotropic breakthrough and in a Zen *kenshō* (enlightenment) experience, there is no figurehead, no worship, no guilt, no self-denial, and no exaltation of an authority greater than oneself. In the minds of my parents and those like them, the drugs were the beginning of a re-distribution of power, largely through self-discovery. Unfortunately, though, it wasn't a cure-all for everything.

My mother and father did planned LSD sessions in the U.S. at different periods before and after Ireland. Eventually, they spent a long time in a castle in Umbria in the summer of 1968, doing more intensive experimentation with friends and like-minded people. There would always be a "straight" watcher, sometimes my father, who made sure things didn't get out of hand. Sometimes a therapist would guide the session, introducing to the subjects an issue that they had struggled with, which in my mother's case was her childhood eczema and the milder eczema that bothered her still. Generally, if a person was on a "good trip," the dose would be piled higher and higher, in order that they have a more transformative experience.

My mother had a particularly awful time. Not long after

she died, my father told me that in Italy they had done experiments, drawing faces on cardboard boxes and calling them
"mother" or "father." When Deborah was presented with her
"mother," she tore the box to shreds like "a wild cat," he said,
as if describing her difficulties would explain her cancer and
her death. To me, it was another in a series of drastic changes,
each linked to the preceding one: LSD, Zen, dying. Though I
understood it intellectually, logic could not apply. No matter
how many adept words were thrown at it, it was still too much
to take in. He added that she often had "bad trips," crying and
screaming through periods of great terror and desolation. He
couldn't believe how she kept going on with it, taking LSD
again and again, piling on the dosage even if she was miserable all through. I had an LSD journal with me in Ireland, one
spiral notebook filled in her loopy hand in pencil. In Ireland, I
read it straight through for the first time, which made the agonizing darkness that she struggled with so much clearer to me.
Annaghkeen, opaque and poetic, was the record that my mother
wanted to leave, but the journals illuminate what it was like to
be Deborah:

*I heard Becky describing something of her childhood and I felt sad
for having no dear things or warm places in my childhood. In previous LSD sessions my experience is often one of desolation and empty
landscapes, while Peter's and others' are full of wild and abundant
if terrible phenomena. I think perhaps because of my struggle with
myself and the eczema, most of my life has been preoccupied with this
terrible thing, and I truly had few experiences that could penetrate my
self-absorption.*

*The landscapes I saw were cold, ashy, desolate. I was in a prairie
of licking flames, but they were cold, and I watched with detachment.
I tried to think of my childhood and a spoke turned, as a wheel.*

Between two spokes a scene paused to be examined, the wheel turned and the next scene came on view, each dull and stiff and peopled with the unfamiliar, pale lifeless green in colour, shockingly empty and boring . . . Urged to find my childhood I said there was nothing to see, and in fact I couldn't find it.

Once, during a session with my father and someone named Jim, she wrote:

Rue was the last form I held on to. She is real, something I can <u>know</u>. *Jim reminded me of the process called Rue, but she stayed intact, if far away. Neither she nor I disintegrated.*

I resented being called a "process" by a well-meaning fool called Jim, while he attempted to apply his theories. He seemed to want to obliterate every connection, every need, every tether my mother had. I seriously question whether that is happiness.

Even so I remember saying, "I always knew I didn't exist. Now it's proven." This in despair. I lay on the sofa and sobbed . . . I felt a stream of liquid running from my eyes and nose, joining in a river flowing to the floor. I had the thought that I would never find the source of my tears, that they were endless, and they were the same as being alive.

My mother believed that her malaise could be cured by encountering the images and feelings that had been imprinted upon her subconscious by experience. If the realities of the past could be routed and re-experienced, they could be exorcised. Since one's personality was a reaction to the early realities, every bodily and psychic need would also be vanquished. Instead, there would be a germ of truth, an underlying place of *pure melting and unimaginable distinctions*, not only for her, but for everyone. It was there, she was sure. If she could cut down through all the layers, her feet would find solid ground.

This applied to the present as well. We used to have terrible fights about my homework, or my clothes, or things that I had done that she perceived as aggressive (that usually weren't, but just kid stuff). Most of these took place in her least favorite room of the house, the kitchen. There was a white recipe box with painted roosters that my eyes would fixate on through these fights. One day, my mother took me through the house on a mission to get rid of things that had bad associations—everything we had looked at or touched while feeling misunderstood and angry. She chose a set of curved highball glasses, a "McCoy's Oil Service" pen, an orange throw pillow from the sofa—more things, because she was fighting with my father as well as me. I remember feeling some reluctance but pointed to the recipe box. "We'll get rid of it," she said, sweeping it into a bag. A milder application of LSD and Zen, this stuck with me. Being able to get rid of an object and its hated associations was delightful. It represented starting over, dropping our emotional baggage by the side of the road and stepping into the light. We were always working on getting rid of the old stuff, paring away the layers, the bad feelings, returning to each other and holding each other tight. It was so easy. For me, this was the lighter side of what she was learning, and consequently I was learning, and is the best thing I know now. Come back to what was authentic, what was lasting, what was true. Though Real Life kept getting in the way, the gift that we had was each other.

Things were vastly more complicated with my father. LSD helped, albeit temporarily, to cut through the discord between them. The LSD sessions helped them get back to their original love, though it never lasted for very long. Until the calamity of illness was upon them, they were really unable to be consistently close. What was lasting were my father's affairs, his long absences, his commitment to his work, her loneliness, her ambition, her struggle with practical matters, and the enduring emotional damage of eczema. Despite her relative detachment from the concept of herself as a beauty, in those years, with a third marriage in trouble, she became increasingly insecure about her looks. During one session, she thought about her flaws:

> All I had to do was think of two scars on my cheek, which are a "flaw" and it triggers a total rejection. Even the word "self" or "me" would cause the phenomenon. I want to leave myself, hear music, join the world, but must stay with this sickening thing. I feel sick; nausea pronounced, headache more severe ... No amount of verbal understanding or self-acceptance will work ...
>
> Peter picked up my arm and said, touching a spot of eczema, "Go into it." I saw the skin redden and thicken and then a mouth opened and I went into it. I remember screaming and wanting to back out and Peter saying for me to go in ... Again the familiar rising scream and rigidity ...

No matter how she tries to pretend otherwise, the eczema is a terrible menacing creature residing inside her, marking her skin, threatening to come alive and tell the secret of her profound inadequacy.

This insecurity was made worse by being married to someone who was unable to stick, who just could not commit, even though he was married. Whenever she gave herself, again, to my father (there were LSD sessions where they re-enacted the marriage ceremony), there was always a sense of futility about it. The dance between "getting out" and "staying in" was something they went through over and over, and she undertook it *personally.* As if in a final valiant bid for him to accept her, and she him, she'd finally be able to accept what was really wrong: herself. It repeated itself on a larger scale in the greater arena of their lives together. Though I know she thought about it privately, the possibility that he might be a major problem in her life didn't manifest itself into any form of action. She was passive, even masochistic. She identified herself as the problem. She went back to him again and again, she continued to try, she remained committed to the cause of the two of them together. On one LSD session, Jim suggested that Peter hold her like a baby in his arms. This went well until it didn't:

I felt that physically we made a perfect circle, with no superfluous extensions—in other words Peter and I were contained in each other . . . I felt his presence continually as if he were there for me almost the whole time. At the end I felt pressure from him for me to quit as if I were doing it all on purpose and he was tired of the game. I wanted it to be over too but knew it wasn't until it was. I felt at certain times that he gave over the whole of himself for me, literally. After the experience Peter was exhausted and I felt not tired at all.

On our walk I began dwelling on other problems, I think because in the Guggenheim museum there was a beautiful lady and I knew how awful I looked and I knew that Peter (part of him) wanted that lady that looked like a jaguar, sleek and beautiful and sure, so I began dwelling morbidly on my flaws, which robbed me a little of the joy and freedom I felt sitting in the park watching the baseball game and the skyline and the clouds.

Like rectangles of sun in a dim, cavernous room, the LSD experiences illuminated a place, a moment, an hour here and there, where she felt unified in mind, spirit, and body. Through LSD, my mother began to believe that the misery of mankind was linked with her personal malaise, each one leading to the other in a tautology. LSD was the key to the way everyone felt, and the cure. It was a tool, a way to find the garden, the original perfect place that we all came from. People might be unshackled from the damage that had been piled upon them by their parents, also victims of a sick society. People might have a chance to be free. She said with pride that she had taken LSD many times when pregnant and that Alex was a perfectly beautiful infant, which indeed he was. She hinted that he was even more beautiful because of the LSD. When the drug was being denigrated in American media, my mother was its great defender, clipping each article that she found, writing letters to various parties in its support. In 1966, the importer of LSD, Sandoz Pharmaceuticals, applied for an "investigational drug" status for psychiatric use but withdrew it because of bad press. In a letter to the company, she wrote:

It is tragic, no less, to suppress its proper use. But this is an old story—of society killing its brightest possibilities, Socrates, Jesus— both introduced to men new and saving ways of regarding themselves and all life. LSD also contains this possibility of seeing ourselves in a new way—it can be a path to real sanity, not the conventions of civilized man. But it takes courage.

As it became apparent that her ability to convey her vision of LSD would be limited, my mother turned in frustration to her own family. During that long ago "acid summer" in Italy, she suggested one day that I take a dose. At the time I was ten years old, leaving the relatively free and magical world of my younger self, hiding behind my face that was turning to stone. I appeared unhappy to her. I might have been unhappy, or I might just have been hiding, or she might have been projecting her unhappiness onto me, or some combination of the three. She thought LSD would help me break through my problems. She asked and, of course, I said yes because that's what they were all doing. With my LSD session scheduled for the following day, I went to bed frightened but also vaguely excited to be doing the wild, adventurous thing that up till then had been reserved for the grown-ups only. I tried not to think about it too much.

In the morning, I woke up in a nervous state and came into the kitchen. My feeling was that I was in their hands and that I'd just give myself over to it, as I'd seen them do so many times, floating around the olive grove or in the surrounding fields, laughing, crying, hugging, looking intently at their hands or a tree or a flower for hours. I gathered up my courage, steeling myself, deciding to be happy about this strange new development. In a way, doing this adult thing might be like graduating from childhood. I couldn't go back on it; otherwise, I'd look afraid, not up to it, not one of the group after all. But a little later on, my father let me know that the LSD session was off. Inasmuch as a ten-year-old agnostic can thank God, I did. I was relieved and a tiny bit disappointed. My mother never spoke of it again.

Away in the Kerry countryside where we were still travelling, the setting was to me still *then*, unchanged. While looking at the narrow road going by or puttering along behind a farmer with a herd of cattle, I could hardly believe that I had made it back more or less intact, and with my own family. My life could have gone any way at all, yet my present circumstances seemed ordinary and peaceful. I felt lucky that none of us had had to struggle with the agonies of the early years. No one was trying to fix anyone or themselves.

Then, as often happens after a comforting assessment of the present, the glaciers made themselves known again. I felt mountain-sized pieces of ice screech and grind against each other, while fault lines opened under the car. A piece of seven-year-old me was left in Ireland, who later became a ten-year-old in New York whose face was expressionless. They are not gone. They are still with me, propping me up at times, undermining me at others, and sometimes just informing me, shedding a light on something I had forgotten but would do well to remember.

Not long before we got on the plane for Ireland, I had a long, intricate dream. In it, my mother had sent me a letter explaining that she hadn't really died. In the dream, she was a figure on the periphery of events; at first, there was only a rumor of her around the town, among my father and stepmother Maria and family friends. Then a letter came for me. In it, my mother said that she was sorry, she'd had to go, and she hoped that I'd had a good life. "I'm sorry, I just couldn't do it" was her statement. I was caught between a wild joy and excitement that she had returned and fear of seeing this woman who had deserted us, who would now be a stranger. Though having terminal cancer is not a choice, a sense of abandonment had stayed with me, maybe because she seemed to have initiated leaving starting with LSD, and then Zen, which in her final years took her away from us for long periods of time. No, it isn't logical, but logic rarely plays a part in a dream.

After having become a mother myself, I was furious with her. How could she? But there she was, planning a return from Canada, where she had hidden out for decades, cool as fresh fallen snow. Then there was a phone call. Somehow, she had gotten the news that I was married and had a child, and somehow, that was completely beside the point. I had a perfect picture of her on the other end of the line, on an old-fashioned phone in a motel room with fifties-style furniture. She conveyed a tepid interest in seeing Emmett and Steve, but it was me she really wanted to see. She had finally made it back; she had pulled through for my sake as much as anything.

In the room, there were no clothes anywhere, no food, no papers—no detritus of living. My mother was out of a Hitchcock film, neat in a crisp cotton shirt and a pencil skirt. I could see her hanging up the phone with a melancholic, satisfied air, and there she remained, for she never materialized again. She was the strange, still woman with a labyrinth of secrets who is none the less empty inside. She had been efficient, but her soul was gone. She was a celluloid figure flickering in an old movie house, living between the dust motes twirling in the projector's rays. She was a certain sort of man's mystery woman, routine while carrying out her desertion, choosing to save herself.

The Girl in the Raincoat

Love's most complex form is between a man and a woman as equals. Perfect opposites, inseparable in their separateness, they embody a paradox, alone in which is found the Whole. For each to be confronted with the other's intention to know himself makes this more terrifying and dazzling than any other relationship.

There was no more to say. I went to bed drunk and destroyed. P came in and after a while, from his bed, came his voice saying he was ashamed of how he had treated Rue. "There is only one way of finding my way back to you, and it is through her."

After a special pub lunch in Wexford, we headed to New Ross to see the Dunbrody emigrant ship tour. The ship is a replica of the original three-masted barque that sailed in the 1840s to the U.S. Actors not three feet away played out the trials of the passengers in the cramped bunk room under the hatches. The voyage took six weeks, and on each trip at least twenty percent of them died. Emmett loved the boat, the water, and the tour especially because he has a theatrical bent and could reach out and touch the players. I'm sure he didn't understand the full story, which is the blessing of the young. A few years older, and he might have internalized that had one of his forebears on his grandfather's side been "buried at sea" on the original Dunbrody or the like, never would I have been lucky enough to meet Steve or have the joy I do in Emmett.

Back at our funky room on the edge of Wexford, Steve plummeted into bed, rapidly approaching flatline, while I hopped over to the store to get the dinner: Pot Noodles and cheese, fizzy water and ice cream cups for them and a Guinness for me. After feeding Emmett, I watched RTE (Raidió Teilefís Éireann) while waiting for him to drift off. The last few nights, I had taken to stealing away to the dining room of our establishment and reading *Annaghkeen* with more attention than I had for years.

I watched as Emmett's lashes lowered over his cheek, a flush blooming there. I noticed again how beautiful he was; in many ways he's the best thing I've ever done. My own response to him surprises me at times. I have never agonized about choices; I am quick and decisive and firm. I am warm but always want to give him space. I have an outsized respect for the force that he is. I try to just step back and see what happens next.

I picked up *Annaghkeen* and my laptop, wending my way to the spare and functional dining room. Being away from all the details of home has given me the time to really read *Annaghkeen* carefully, and of course Ireland was the perfect place. But being in the setting of the book, as well as getting closer to Galway every day, had given my mother's words a new and disconcerting slant. I was discovering and remembering things and putting them together in a new storyline that wasn't aligned with what I had previously chosen to remember.

From the dining room, I watched the soft light withdraw from the garden—late, as the sun doesn't really begin going down in August until 9:30 or so. The chairs were uncomfortable, the light diffuse, the humming blue monitor of my laptop the only illumination. There wasn't a sound, except from a marked-up green book. I thought of my mother's Zen challenge about not thinking for three breaths and tried to clear my head. We are always at work, summing up ourselves and others, deciding whether we are good or bad, lucky or unlucky, putting up a flimsy structure that we cling to that separates us from the riches that surround us—as well as protects us from what we fear. I struggled to leave that structure far behind and just take things as they were—*Annaghkeen* without its frayed dust jacket, invaded with Post-its. A plain room washed in milky light, empty but for me, with four round tables, a rack of tourist brochures, the breakfront set up for tomorrow morning with canisters of cereal.

Removing distractions had been the point of this trip, and to try to let light in on the past. On the inevitable conclusion of Real Life in all its forms—a reigning theme throughout *Annaghkeen*—well, how could I argue? On the subject of Real Life, I *liked* it—my Real Life anyway. At that moment I missed even the dregs of it, the inane distractions that I was mostly taken up with at home. I felt adrift among these old personae.

Annaghkeen fell open to page stuck with a Post-it. Back at home, while skimming the book, I had marked the page because it irked me. In 1965, when attending the Galway races, my parents were pulled over in their VW by two Garda (policemen). Having snagged some Americans, the young Garda puffed up authoritatively and commanded them to produce their visas. They didn't have them.

We pretended surprise since he was absolutely right to arrest us. Haven't we been sinning for years?

How clearly I understood Josef K. As long as it's unspecified, the case will hold, the verdict is guilty. If only "they" would accuse one of "something" one could fight to the death in earnest.

Of what am I guilty?

I am guilty of not totally agreeing to being alive.

Why not?

Because then of course, I would agree to die, implicit in the first state, and to this I do not agree. It is simply not safe to be alive. But this failure to agree is troubling, for there seem to be no alternatives.

I grabbed my pen and wrote in the margins of the book: Is the choice, then, to simply withdraw?

Oh, I have my reasons for having failed, but they are secrets.

Fascinating, what are they?

If they were revealed they would be seen for what they are, excuses.

Always making it your fault. Maybe it wasn't your fault.

The secrets give personality to the person. In creating them he delineates his shape, and thus presents himself to the world—

One's shape can be known without secrets—unless one is incapable of being direct!

The personality (its Latin root is persona, meaning a mask) informed by secrets, distinguishes one from all others. Is this not necessary to survival? Otherwise, how could one be found? Who would come to the rescue?

But there *is* a real person, and they *will* disappear behind a mask; *I* am a real person, for example, and I don't care what the Latin root is. What good is disappearing?

And too, this personality, designed and put on, gives the impression of not-life, therefore that which cannot die . . .
Yet breathing becomes increasingly difficult through the mask, and death is not what I had imagined.

My poor Mama. You loved it when I still called you Mama, even when I was older. *Mama*, said softly and sweetly, was my calling card, when I couldn't get through to you and nothing else would work. Yet we, your darling sweet babies, had to grow up. We were transforming from the "Beauty of essentials, Perfectly turned in round wonder of the world" into just two more exhausting people.

Thinking of Emmett, back in the room asleep, I wondered at his innocence. He is a self-confident, observant child who doesn't worry about new places or being without us and always has something to say. He's fun to talk to, and he likes to argue, and does so for the sake of the exercise as well as to get what he wants. He often sounds much older than he is. But I never forget that he is a child and will be for a long time. I especially don't forget it because in my youth I was verbal, good at mimicry, and good at reaching into my stores of common sense to fit the moment. I "saw" what was going on, and I often said it, which made me seem like something I wasn't. I was more delicate and malleable than anyone understood. I try to remember that with any child, especially my own.

The yellowing pages with their cryptic paragraphs swam before me. Her "reasons," her "guilt," and her "failure." An odd dual sensation swept over me—examining my mother's quandaries as an adult, along with a visceral dread at being caught up in the gears of everything as a kid. Of course, I no longer *was* a kid, but the child I was, was still there.

My friend Jackson Braider, there as a boy at Annaghkeen, said, "She loved men and they loved her, but she was confounded by them." Yes, she did love them in a particularly old-fashioned and romantic way—in that her *fate* was in play in every relationship she had. But she chose difficult men. There was always a struggle in it, some kind of war going on, not just with my father—almost every man she had ever been with. Her brother Kenny said that in her younger years the beautiful Deborah had beaux coming and going, and she tossed them away like corncobs over a fence. She preferred it, he said, because she liked to "leave first." But that wasn't always the case. Her sisters Mary and Nathalie let me know that she was pregnant on her first wedding day (as well as her second, with me) and that she pressured Bill Deacon to marry her despite the fact that they were ill-suited for each other. That was the marriage to get out of the house. A woman not in college, not "protected" by man or marital status was considered a bit of a scandal—difficult for me to imagine, but not all that long ago. Those were still the days of special "ladies' hotels" in cities, the only accommodation in their circles considered fitting for a woman alone.

Coming out of such a conventional mold, it must have been quite a surprise, not least to Deborah herself, that she had burned through two marriages by the age of thirty-two. In her journal, there's a funny passage where she has to qualify for the FHA loan for the house we lived in before she met my father. The lawyer asks for proof that she hasn't changed her name in ten years. She cannot provide it because there were three names: Deborah Love, Deborah Deacon, and Deborah Pollock (so far). The lawyer needs the dates of her marriages and divorces, and she cannot remember one of them. She wrote that his smile turned to a smirk, and that suddenly *he had the power.* He had "the goods" on her—she was all wrong and always had been.

The idea that she couldn't measure up to the fifties standard of womanhood was a consistent regret. By her third marriage, it began to dawn on her that she could just do things her own way. My father had made her financially secure, enabling her to have staff to take care of the things she wasn't interested in doing and opening up her time. Though the extra help removed her to some extent from her children, I can't resent the assistance. I remember her as happiest in her study with the fireplace painted white, working on her journals and poems or editing a draft on the daybed, plucking her eyebrow in concentration. It always seemed that she was in her element among books and language.

My father's ambition and hers were a lot alike, though my father got started much earlier. He knew himself to be a writer from the age of sixteen. He wrote fast, he was charming, and he made sure he was connected with people who could help him along. He worked incredibly hard. He already had a short bibliography when he met her, and he was determined to take his success much further. When they married, he knew that he would place huge demands on himself and everyone around him.

Notwithstanding the extra help, my mother struggled. As well as the running of the house, most domestic arrangements fell to her, including visits with kids from his first marriage. But her intellectual confidence overrode any reticence she might have had about claiming her own time to write and study. And as my father became more famous, it never occurred to her to recede into the background. She would not have been content to bask in his reflected glory. Many people saw them as being in some sort of competition, like a pair of twins. Early on, people said that she was the luminous one, the adventurer, the star. She often said that marriage to my father was like being "two kids in a sandbox." He was always worried that she might have more, that she might *be* more, that in certain ways he was begrudging and stingy.

When my father went away, she was as flummoxed by ordinary things in his absence as she was overtaken by them in his presence. His workaholic tendencies at home and her long periods alone caused them to blow apart and come together emotionally and physically, over and over again. Dramatic, heated, spitting-mad fights turned into weeks of wintry chill, where they didn't speak unless necessary and spent most of the time in their separate studios, working. Whether together or apart, they were always on the verge of some sort of ending. The end of them? The end of freedom? The end of what? There was a great deal at stake. Like most children, I felt more than I could rationally understand. It was like watching two comets collide and getting caught in the center of the explosion, then blowing out into space in a shower of sparks.

In the post-*Annaghkeen* years, the drama increased, and how precipitous it all felt. We were encircled by a feeling of terrible vacancy. Our village got very cold in the winter, the corn and potato fields that surrounded the house went into deep freeze. Way out on the end of Long Island, there were periodic ice storms and blizzards and power outages. Long before death made a visit, how morose and dark Sagaponack already was. The agonizing barrenness, the exhausted, irritated Christmases. The power struggles, the wearing down, the giving in, the hugs, the music. The desperation, the refusals, the battles, the betrayals. The emptiness in between, my God, the emptiness. The colors, scarlet and brown; the materials, velvet and corduroy. The cold dinners, with no one talking. The chilly tinkle of the dinner bell. My father, needing so much to be away from us. Needing us to be there, but needing to be away from us. Never really needing to be with us. Never needing me. Her needing me though. Needing me to fall back on when he gave out or left for another long trip.

There were a lot of feelings swirling around his leaving, the long goodbyes, and the anticipation of his return. These had different soundtracks—her face would soften, and she'd hum along to the car radio, chewing the Trident gum she liked in the afternoons to stave off hunger pangs. "Raindrops Keep Falling on My Head," where the singer tries to piece his life together, was one, as was the sad romance of Simon and Garfunkel's "Scarborough Fair." Those were played more when he was gone. "Do You Believe in Magic?" was another, completely different thing. When the Lovin' Spoonful was on the stereo, my father was home, and things were on the upswing. I can't listen to "Do You Believe in Magic?" without crying. It was a theme to those carefree days when resentments had been chucked out the window and they had called a truce. An intense sort of relief came flooding through the house; a bright, blindingly sunny day after months of gloom. The future suddenly opened up into straight lines where one could sail with no end after being hopelessly tied up and stagnant. This particular joy had a taint of madness because everything, of course, would get tied up again. As a child, it was irresistible for me not to believe along with them. The party was on, the mood was beautiful, and they were smiling together; sometimes all three of us wound up together, in a hug, in the living room, with not a care in the world.

Another song was "Leaving on a Jet Plane," by Peter, Paul and Mary. This one always marked a departure, yet another sad and melancholy ending in a house suffused with them. I remember one morning in particular, when he was leaving for a months-long trip. I suspect that it was him that put "Leaving on a Jet Plane" on the stereo. I came down to the living room to find them wrapped in an embrace so concentrated they didn't hear my footsteps. The squabbles and petty differences of the weeks before had dissolved away. They had been returned, once again, to each other, only this time a softer, more sober light shone through the house, a mellow sunset instead of bright midday. The twinge of sadness was because he was leaving, but there was a deeper reason, more to do, somehow, with fate. He wasn't responsible for what was going to happen—that while he was away there would be other women. She knew it, he knew it. I knew it. The fact was as thick as honey in the air. Though it galled her, the pattern had been established. I can still feel my mother making use of her own desertion; I can feel how her impending loneliness contributed to the intensity. And I can remember how she retaliated, somewhat half-heartedly, looking up old boyfriends when he was away and sometimes right under his nose.

What was it like at the beginning? There was hope and a great deal of love. I know there was because I was right in the middle of it. By the time I was ten, the story of my mother (wife number two) had played out and, in that cavernous loveless house, was fast coming to a conclusion. I could see it and feel it, wending its way toward us silently, as if on hawk's wings.

The *Annaghkeen* summer was still quite a few years before this. The sixties hadn't geared up yet, nor had my father's career, or the intensity of the strife between them. Back then, my father was still looking for what they half-jokingly called "the girl in the raincoat" who waited on a "dark rainy night at a bus stop," an image that I love despite that his search for this elusive creature was so destructive. Unlike many of the women who vied for and got his attention, "the girl in the raincoat" was the only one *he* sought. He found her a few times, and I think that my mother was one manifestation, until some real facet of hers blew the picture. My mother tried to describe the nature of her own former incarnation:

Who is the girl in the raincoat? P. says she is lost innocence but I think she is a yearning for perfection (perhaps the same thing). Romance demands parting and parting is sorrow, because sorrow is for endings it is the deepest feeling we know.

My mother, trying to learn from the competition, was toughening herself. She tried to comprehend this fantasy and where it was taking them. But "the girl in the raincoat," an expression of my father's deep restlessness, would not really transform into something other than what she was—a catastrophe. My mother, as usual, took it upon herself. She tried to puzzle out her own part in a marriage, or any woman's:

She has tried to please him, but it is freedom he wants; to eat his cake and have it, to take the woman along. But for this she too must be free, without guilt; without guilt there can be no penance. And two are left exposed. She could step from behind his back, and look with her own eyes at the starry night, and they would both be relieved and glad to be friends.

As in the LSD journals, there is the same sense of longing to be free of responsibility and guilt. But how is it that the guilt is hers? And how, by freeing herself of it, can she absolve him of *his* guilt? In the dining room, I wandered around, wondering how, in her future utopia, his cheating would no longer matter. Was she that idealistic? Was I being too literal? Were the sixties that long ago? I thought that all of this must go back to Adam and Eve and the apple—things I had little context for. I was grateful not to, and despite my frustration, I had my mother to thank for rejecting it as best she could and then shielding me from it.

In Dublin, while visiting my father's friends from his first marriage, Donald and Carol Braider, my mother and father were about to separate. As usual, I was caught in the middle. (Earlier, Don and Carol had offered to take me for a whole year, as their daughter was in boarding school, and then scaled it down to just one month.)

A heavy atmosphere seemed to invade the climate of the room, the pressure felt by the sudden disappearance of our relevance to each other.

The Braiders offered to keep Rue while we went on a tour of Scotland and Wales in August. Surprised, I burst into tears. How did they know? Everything was wrong. Everyone was on trial, and all found wanting; nobody accepted anybody. P came to the door at the sounds of disintegration. Luke crept down from the attic with Christopher and Jackson to listen from the hall. Rue, everybody's scapegoat, slept soundly at the far end of the house.

"Maybe it would be a good idea to take Rue," I sobbed. "She should live among people who like her, who don't use her for their own rages. Who are only attacking me through her."

This morning in the bus as I sat with Rue cradled in my arms, a voice (my father's) hissed epithets which went unanswered.

Now I addressed the voice. In the flood of tears floated the debris of abuse, particles of rage and outrage. P stood, angry and abashed, where he had entered the room.

"Why do you tell me all this in front of Carol and Don?"

I said they knew it anyway and I had said it a thousand times to him.

I would give him Alexander, who was made from us both, and take Rue and go. Good-by, Good-by.

Though *Annaghkeen* is filled with separations large and small, the Dublin chapter is the most straightforward treatment the disintegrating situation gets in the entire book. It's an attempt at honesty—at least, about the seriousness of the moment where my mother spoke again about leaving. My brother Alex was less than a year old, at home with Nanny Frances in New York. He was seven years old when she died and doesn't have a clear memory of her. Among scant recollections, he has also been left *Annaghkeen*, including most unfortunately this passage. As I've often said to him, he was adored by our mother and all of us. He was a ray of light shining into the general gloom, and that was only more so as he grew up.

The passage really has more to do with them than me or an eleven-month-old baby. I often wonder why they stayed together (well past this episode; indeed, to the very end years later), and I think it was a mixture of a real love for each other, as well as a certain weariness with *themselves*, with three divorces between them already and children bouncing between houses. There was at least the dawn of a genuine desire to not tear everything up again. Though the focus was always upon *their* fate, there was more at stake now.

In the dining room of my B and B, a row of Irish tourism posters goggled out at me absurdly, *Céad Míle Fáilte* and *Erin go Bragh*. The feeling of loneliness that had marked this night sharpened. Suddenly, I felt unmoored again, much as I had back then. In *Annaghkeen* and the LSD journals, there were ghosts of things, subtleties, strong undercurrents that pertained only to me residing in the spaces between the words, the interstices between the pages. Things not written down. The yellowing pages with their sentences swam before me. ... *Weaving myself whole again with strands of information, she is a complete creature ... Rue was the last form I held on to. She is real, something I can know ... Maybe it would be a good idea to take Rue ...*

Why was I sitting in this bed-and-breakfast way out in Wexford in the middle of the night by the light of ghosts? I was involved with and affected by my parents, as most children are, but it was more than that. After the *Annaghkeen* summer, everything had gotten considerably worse. I can call it worse only in retrospect because at the time I just went along, not knowing how bad it was. Just thinking it was normal.

In 1969 at my progressive school, I had few friends. The kids made fun of the hand-me-down clothes my mother liked for me and called me "Rheumatism" and "Rubella." A boy I liked decided I had the cooties, and then everyone said I had the cooties and wouldn't get near me. I didn't know how to fit in, and I was so discouraged I didn't try. My mother, caught up in her own drama, hadn't a realistic sense of what was going on. The happiest part of my life was Alex, then about four years old, whom I lavished with attention every chance I got.

As I re-read *Annaghkeen*, I also remembered with newfound clarity that when my father was gone, my mother and I slept together, and not without intimacy. I don't remember Alex ever being there. There was never anything overtly sexual, but it was very physical. We were too close. Many people said it then, and many more didn't say it but thought so. I could tell they disapproved. Maybe there was an air about us, a way that we were involved that was visible. When my father was away, we slept together, hugging through long winter nights, all entwined together under her electric blanket. We took oil baths in the huge square tub and washed each other's backs and hugged afterward, naked, the house cavernous and cold around the warm nucleus of the bathroom. I remember that our bodies fit together perfectly. Hot and oily from the bath, we'd stand on the white carpet next to the tub, completely and passionately entwined for minutes at a time. I could feel her ferocious need and responded with a sort of flowering. Within those hugs, I went someplace deep inside myself where there were black, exploding stars—silent, unending stars that were a part of me and her and no one else. No one, no one, no one would ever take them away. I found a timeless solace from the misery of my life at school and the fundamental emptiness of life at home. And I knew she did too.

But, of course, the light of day did come. The troubles at school went on, I was unpopular and had terrible grades, and home was no sanctuary. Then there was my mother. Blinking on and off, with a divine and ever more precarious love. Did she know what was going on with me? She never asked. Did she wish to heal me? No. Was she trying to heal herself? Probably. I knew enough to *try* not to need her; I knew that something wasn't right. The feeling I had with her was borrowed, or *I* had been borrowed, for a purpose that hadn't much to do with me. It was really, essentially, about *them*. Still, because of my age, this detached sense I had of it did not prevent it from being overwhelming. The in-between parts, the chill between her and my father and the passionate heat, the way he and I were traded out for each other in the bedroom depending on whether he was engaged with her, or even home at all, the silence and emptiness in the house was so unbearable that at twelve years old I went to boarding school in England of my own volition. It was as far away as I could get without having a language problem. (Also, I had seen the movie *Oliver!* at least ten times and read all of Frances Hodgson Burnett. I thought England would be peopled with adults horrible and kindly, and charismatic orphans with elaborate backstories. I was not entirely wrong.)

How much did my father know? I'm not sure, but he always did have a sense of my mother going back and forth between us. We were indeed a triangle. He might have chosen to not completely understand. He might have put it aside in his mind. After she died, he said that I would be free, that I would be better off without her. I didn't agree with that at all. But until I sat there so many years later—with my uncomfortable memories and forensic reading of *Annaghkeen*—I still didn't have the full picture.

At the end of the Dublin chapter, things were beginning to simmer down. My mother and my father did decide to leave me with the Braiders while she and my father, along with Luke, took a short visit to Mount Melleray Abbey—my mother's idea. When they got to the abbey, they found that she wasn't allowed on the advertised tour. She wrote of feeling a familiar pang of panic *at being excluded for being a woman*. She follows up to say that the pang was dismissed by *the director of human relationships in my head*, while my father and Luke disappeared into the forbidden territory.

Sitting there in the dining room, I remembered the phrase. The sun had gone completely down now. I noticed only because the daughter of the owners came in, apologetic as she stocked the refrigerator with butter and milk from a box. I tried to be polite, but I felt about a hundred miles away.

I thought of the story my mother used to tell me when I was small: There was a woman, and she was lost, very lost and sad. And then along came a beautiful child who saved her. "Who was that child?" I'd ask. "You," she'd say. As I grew up, the passing years were an occasion for sorrow—hers, and consequently, mine. Something I had brought was being taken away. Yet *I* was still there. That night in the dining room, the sequence of events I read and remembered fell into a pattern. These things were in the distant past, yet I saw for the first time how it all hung together, and it wasn't favorable to me. Suddenly, I saw that all the people helping her in her quest to reach perfection—my father, Carol and Don Braider, the audience out on the lawn, the LSD coach Jim, and maybe many others—believed that what she needed to be free of was *me*. By the time I left for boarding school, she had already been leaving for a good while. It all culminated for me one winter day in 1969.

She was in her study upstairs, her desk covered with open books, a cup of hot chocolate in her hand, and some heavy classical music playing at a low volume in the background. I was standing at the corner of the desk. I will never forget it. She said, "I don't love you as much as I used to." The words rang out and bounced from the white walls and the white brick fireplace back toward me. I hadn't done anything wrong; it wasn't a punishment. It was more an announcement of a new and permanent development. She made no attempt at an explanation. There was no regret. There was (surprisingly for her) no remorseful retraction and hugs and kisses. Then or later. Creating an explanation for this remark was up to me.

Now, with *Annaghkeen* open in front of me, I considered it. Emmett was not that much younger than I had been on that day. How could she have said this to me? To coin her phrase, *the director of human relationships in my head* at that age was just getting into gear. As I attempted to explain this comment to myself over the next years—indeed, decades—my *director of human relationships*, such as it was, was strained to the limits of capability. I could feel that she meant it. She was pulling away. First, I thought it was my fault. Later, I had a sense that she thought she was doing me a favor because she believed her love for me was toxic. Then another facet developed: She believed that her new path to salvation (Zen) would not have a place for me, and she needed to clear the way.

On that memorable afternoon, I didn't respond. I hadn't anything to say. Instead, I left her study. I "thought" the way an eleven-year-old would. I shoved it under the rug for the "director" to deal with, very slowly. My mother was failing to see that her love for me had no beginning or end, or my mother had gone temporarily crazy. Or my mother was trying to straighten herself out, and I was just caught in it. My mother was trying to do me a favor. She was desperate. She did not remember her love for me was the center of all things and could not change.

Over time, I gathered any strands of wisdom that I might have actually had and wove them together. That early love would have to be hidden away. It would be alluded to at times as a sort of undercurrent, but I would no longer actively need it. It would have to be recategorized as something definitive that had happened long ago at the genesis of things, like the red-hot core of a volcano that exploded once and changed the terrain around it. It was now untouchable. I would not require the usual supports because they simply weren't there. I would have to leave—and so I did, in the fall, for Cobham Hall in England.

Around me on four walls, the Irish tourism posters surveyed the scene. Even with the barebones style in which we had to travel, this trip had begun as a somewhat romantic idea. I had been little taken with the family mystique. So many people wanted to know about us, especially about the early years of my father's career—oh so fascinating, oh so glamorous. In my mind, I had seen it as *they* might have envisioned it: inky images of the Irish countryside, us bumbling along in the red VW, whiling away afternoons in the lap of ruins. There was an island weighted with symbolism in a lake ringed with castles.

There was a famous, charismatic father who would go on to an extraordinary life and career. There was a lovely, caring mother whom I'd once had almost to myself. I saw myself following her thoughts, following her footsteps then, and following them again now in the present day.

I was arrogant when I began this quest. I believed that I would control the story. I *could*, after all. Nothing would go into it that I couldn't create or re-create. But I hadn't been prepared for what would be exposed under scrutiny. My father often said, "I shouldn't have had kids. I'm not that good a father." But still, he did accumulate children (and wives) like stubs of the No. 2 pencils he used to write with. And my mother, saying such a thing to a child of eleven, in order to push her own "process" forward. Or maybe it was true—maybe she was finished with me. Especially in light of now being a mother, I was horrified at how caught up with themselves they were, and how inadvertently cruel.

Hell's Bells

. . . the artist invents himself from the sound he hears deep in the heart's core. For Yeats, Sligo and the Irish myths are the country of his provenance. Dublin and History are Joyce's. Kafka and Hesse crossed and recrossed the empty continent of the soul, for in Germany there was nobody home.

Here we were in Dublin, heart of what has been called the "Celtic Tiger." After so many ancient forests, tours, and country roads, we might've needed a break from the extraordinary. In any case, our hotel—a seedy, mid-range toiler called the Jury's Inn—has provided it. Its north-facing brick façade rises like a prison wall from the sidewalk, directly across the street from Christ Church Cathedral. Our soot-tinted windows look out over a concrete expanse, broken by four straggly trees. Groups of rough types loiter outside in the glow of the lobby lights, cans of Guinness jammed into the back pockets of their jeans, whooping and hooting and hollering at all hours.

Dublin is ancient, with narrow, mostly one-way streets that make driving here, if one isn't in the know, like being a fly caught in a sticky web. Maybe it would have been easier to relinquish the car, but the trip was planned like this so we could go on straight from Dublin to Galway. They don't believe in street signs here either. Occasionally, there was an old sign nailed to the corner of a building, but otherwise I felt on my own trying to decipher which right turn I had just made off what square, the pile of maps useless, and my husband basically uninterested in maps anyway. I say one way, and he says another, and the proof is whether we've gotten any closer, or dare I say, arrived. Usually, upon the miraculous moment a little revision work takes place, *Wow, glad we made that left on the corner, yea?* asks the victorious one. But in Dublin, none of this applies. Because no one knows where they are or gets any closer. When we floated up in front of the hotel, it was as if on some sort of benevolent and merciful cloud.

As we were checking in, Emmett was fascinated by a group of women who had apparently just walked out of *Alice in Wonderland*. Through the big revolving door, we could see the tips of their pink rabbit ears over the backs of their chairs, the rest of the party arrayed around like a psychedelic sunflower. The ladies were drinking cosmopolitans, mimosas, big round snifters of cognac and red wine. Steve went up to the room, but Emmett wanted to tarry awhile. Emmett has big hazel eyes with long dark lashes. He was wearing his favorite orange shorts and a too-small striped T-shirt from which his belly stuck out adorably. He held fast to his spot at the periphery of their circle, waiting for his explanation. Eventually, their conversation petered out, and a pretty brunette said to him, "It's a hen pohtty, luv" with that same soft "t" that everyone seems to have. She introduced herself as Stacy. Her friend Diana, almost swallowed up by the enormous armchair next to her, was getting married on Saturday at Slane Castle outside the city.

"What do you do at a hen party?" I asked.

"Everything she won't be able to do after Saturday," came the brunette's quick reply followed by raucous laughter.

I looked down at my six-year-old, a smile of pure sunshine breaking over his face at the merriment.

"Oh, a *bachelorette* party," I followed, never having been to one. I quickly assessed the situation; it was only about six o'clock. I gathered my courage to pry, "What will you do later?"

Her mouth turned down a little at the corners as if to hold back the information. "Going out clubbing . . ." she said.

I detected a ripple of anticipation. Somewhere among them was a long-held breath that was slowly beginning to exhale, like a pinprick in a gas hose. This divulgence about clubbing was only half the story. Then there was a collective pulling in so as to not let the breath out now but save it for later. There were a myriad of reasons. It was dangerous, I was a stranger, Emmett was too young, it was too early (people still rushing by the hotel on their way home from work), it was too late, and we weren't peers. Had I by some chance gone to school with them, in the same town, and gone through life with them, I would know.

I reached for words, "Ah yes, clubbing. I used to go in New York. Lost some hearing probably . . ." I joked, wanting to bring the pragmatic back into the fantastical atmosphere.

Was Emmett thinking that these women were all in chains of some kind, or due to be in them, and were making the most of their freedom while they could? My mother hated these sorts of cookie-cutter rituals, as they made her feel trapped. My up-bringing was so unconventional that my friends married late and sporadically, if at all. The prevailing mood in the lobby told me that these women, far away from husbands or boyfriends, were supported by each other in relation to what was going to happen. Or not happen. In a tightly woven system, this was a way to get a memory. Emmett, perceiving only that these women were part rabbit, saw it only as some sort of a fairy tale. And perhaps it was.

"Want to touch the ears?" said Stacy, bending her head just so. Emmett touched the tip of one pink ear, sampling its strange plastic fur with his fingers. "Here, look!" she said, bending both ears at right angles and hunching her shoulders and making a face. Emmett laughed, as we all did.

I wished them well, noticing that the bride especially was charmed by him, as all women who want to have babies are. On the way up to our room, I wondered what rabbit ears had to do with hens.

I could tell that Dublin was an improvement for Steve by the spring in his step, his suitcase rolling along briskly. Ever Irish and taciturn, Steve rarely announces his moods or gives any credence to them. His guarded brown eyes pretty much say that moods will come and moods will go, but he isn't going to go so far as get involved with them. He's like a bus driver, turning the big bus wheel slowly, eyes straight ahead. People and things will persist and people and things will die or become obsolete, and so will feelings and moods. He strives for a profundity beyond all of this. Perhaps it's the combination of his Catholic upbringing and his Zen training, and he has hit some sort of sweet spot between the two. Above all, he wants to remain unruffled, and I think but don't know for sure that a calm demeanor helps keep him that way inside.

Steve wouldn't admit it, but he loved Dublin. How could it be, I wondered. He doesn't drink and doesn't like to be around drinking or crowds, which Dublin is full of. Public drinking seemed to go on night and day in front of the hotel, around the cathedral, and in every park and street corner. People stand around with cans stuck into every available pocket of their clothing. The entire country links Guinness and liquid things to put into your body as naturally as milk and babies. I remembered Patrick back at Muckross taking our picture with the carriage and horse, asking Max to "Smile for the picture" with a pint of Guinness as his reward . . . Guinness for Patrick, Guinness for the horse, Guinness the corrective to anything that might seem out of kilter. Got a cold? Have a Guinness. Feeling blue? Have a Guinness. Work week done? Work week beginning? Lunch? Breakfast?

The Guinness had to be budgeted in for me—a few a week. Perhaps a few more in Dublin. But even here we had to try to stick with it. Now three-quarters of the way through our trip, we had still managed to spend only one hundred dollars (about seventy euro) per day. That was for any sights we wanted to see, food, transportation and gas, pub or chippy nights and noodle nights (last night was pub night; at the Jury's Inn, it was noodle night). We have been able to stick to this plan in large part thanks to a conglomeration called Unilever. What is Unilever? A British multinational that makes Pot Noodle. What is Pot Noodle? Our lifeline.

I tried to laugh about it. Unilever in contrast to life in 1965, living on fresh eggs and milk and poultry from the neighboring Mulloy farm, while eating out at Ashford Castle, and blasting all over the country in our red VW with nary a thought for the costs. I thought about those country people, struck by the fine and elegant figures of my parents—betting at the Galway races, or buying groceries at King's solitary little shop up at the crossroads, my mother's wallet flush with Irish pounds. We were a marvel (didn't we have anything better to do?), and they were marvelous to us, by turns friendly and reserved, with the quality of old souls. But that was then, and things had changed. The U.S. economy was much weaker now, and Ireland was one of the strongest nations in the EU, furthering the crippling effects upon the dollar. Dublin was buzzing. Amid all the excitement, we counted our euros, parsing them out cautiously.

Pot Noodle is available in three sizes: Standard, King, and Mini. Since it was a meal for us, we always got the king size, and that's mostly all that was available anyway. Though we did try all the flavors: Chicken and Mushroom (Steve and Emmett's favorite), Sticky Rib, Tikki Masala, Christmas Dinner, Doner Kebab, Seedy Sanchez, and Bombay Bad Boy. Tikki Masala and Bombay Bad Boy were my favorites. You would think my choices wouldn't go well with cheese, but you would be mistaken.

The Seedy Sanchez slogan is, "Eet's dirty and you want it." The TV advertisements were hilarious, depicting uptight, upper-crust Brits at high-end restaurants or in their homes over white tablecloths and silver, privately longing for Pot Noodles, eyes rolling back like minstrel players, fighting the tide of their own desires, dreading the fallout, savoring the thrill once they and the Pot Noodles come together. Pot Noodle is also called the "Slag of all Snacks."

So what came first, people's perception that Pot Noodle is somehow dirty and base, or Unilever's ad campaign? I really don't know. But I do know there is something dirty about Pot Noodle.

First, you'll rarely eat it at a table, so not much conversation will be had. All you need to make a Pot Noodle is a kettle and a spoon. This will most likely be a plastic spoon. At the Jury's Inn in the linty belly button of Dublin, we didn't even have chairs to sit on. We couldn't eat on the beds because Emmett was still too fumble-fingered. We assembled the basics: three Pot Noodle, cheese in the red wax from the breakfast buffet, pears or apples (usually hard), or bananas (usually green), a copy of *USA Today* from the lobby spread out on the floor to make a table.

Emmett loved it. The newspapers, the TV flickering, and the three of us cooking it up together, the foil pack of powder torn open and poured over the dehydrated product, then the broken-up cheese stirred in, then the boiling water (*stir well*), then the little paper lid on, with a shoe or a book on top to keep it down (*Annaghkeen* works well) for the five-minute steep. Then off comes the lid, another stir, and voilà, you have something that looks like the Western world's first noodle experiment in the sixteenth century, or noodles cooked in sewage. Then the taste. Depending on the flavor, somewhere between powdered Fritos and curry, or powdered Fritos with freeze-dried chicken. Mixed in with pulverized bouillon and small green things that might be onion-related.

That's a fourteen-euro dinner for three people. Six for the Pot Noodle, four for my beer, and four for juice and soda and maybe an ice cream for Emmett. I got the Guinness along with the hoods, lining up at the shop on the corner. While I waited, I thought of the typical Irish family in Galway back then, how they would surely be laughing now. I laughed too. I didn't feel compromised by the restrictions. In my limited experience I've found that luxury is overrated. Cosseted with comfort and surrounded by only beauty, edges dull, contrasts fade—the pampered one turns into an unfeeling cream puff in an uninteresting land. My father, also fond of this view, always said that an excessively pleasant existence turns quickly to rot.

In Dublin, we were grateful to be in one place and not have to drive. We were worn down by the miles that had flown under our wheels—Shannon, Dingle, Killarney, Bantry, Youghal, Wexford—staying nowhere longer than three nights and driving a good deal of every day—rattling, buzzing, flying along. At a certain point, one breaks through some kind of barrier and begins to disintegrate chromosomally. For adults, the feeling can be like a high, an altered state similar to jet lag, mixed in with too much foreign everything—money, people, mores, culture. Not enough of our habits, having to develop new habits: Emmett and I our journals, Steve his travel guitar, Pot Noodle nights and pub nights, or our favorite tunes on the car radio, "SexyBack" and "I Don't Feel Like Dancin.'" We said "feckin' hell" on our way to the "chippy," and sometimes things were really "grand," and sometimes they were "desperate." Stay in a foreign country for long enough, and there is no choice but to just give in. Along the way, we had told people that we were headed to a castle called Annaghkeen in Lough Corrib that I lived near when I was seven. Ahh, they'd say—things have changed a lot since then. Well, *of course* they have, I'd think, while dreading how right they were, and how different it might be. In Dublin, we were suddenly so close. Cong, one of the main settings of *Annaghkeen*, was a two-hour drive away, straight across the middle of the country.

In August, night comes late. As we settled into our generic pod, the cathedral bells came chiming and pealing through the room. Steve wanted to shut the windows because the bells interfered with the news. He wanted to be corralled by the four walls, the encroaching furniture, and the television, surrounded on all sides and boxed in. He liked the honeycomb aspect of the Jury's Inn, in the beehive of the city, its turbulent, restless energy compressing him from without. While I wanted the big sky, the same endless sky as the bums have. I'd hear the bells and want to take flight on them, billows and billows of bells, way up in the lofty pure gray of clouds.

As usual, Emmett was in his own world. I watched him picking up trucks and toys and tossing them aside, flipping through his picture books, looking out with me at the cathedral all lit up and the bums falling around the little scraggly trees. He was like an errant cop, fiddling with the phone, dialing a few numbers, making Frisbees out of drink coasters, flinging them at Steve, then back to the window, waiting for the woman out there to scream with laughter in that particular way she has. I love Emmett and am totally exhausted by him. He is looking for a miracle, he's looking for magic, he's looking for something to happen that tells him he is special, that tells him he won't have to face the limits that he fears. The magic he seeks will absolve him and anoint him and let him be a child for a little longer. The magic is at the same time another kind of limit, a thing to have to commit to, but if it is of his own making, he'll accept it because he's that type. Most especially, the magic will tell him who he is.

While I watched him, I was reminded of my mother and father, and to some degree myself. We were and are driven to re-create the world and the self by any available means. More often than not, this is spurred by a deficit. An artist is unfinished as a child is unfinished. In their history, somewhere along the chain, links were missed, leaving them in a state of flux. Artists are constantly forming and re-forming their worlds in search of defining particularities. They must make something new, pin something down and be able to say, at least for a time, "That's me" or "That's the world I live in," which are basically the same thing. The artist must transcend, make something original out of the raw stuff, write the paragraph that is greater than words standing alone, paint the picture that takes the mind of the viewer into another realm. Each remains a strange hybrid of the adult who must create a version of themselves and the headstrong child. Their specialness will never be relinquished—their insecurity won't allow it. Even if it costs them dearly, the artist deliberately refuses to understand the limits of time, or themselves, or what other people are willing to do for them, and especially, what other people need from them.

My own experience has shown that when artists have children, they are not compelled by the practical needs of the new arrivals. My father never thought, "I would do anything for this creature," a self-awareness most new parents naturally come to. He had to work at it manually, if he worked at it at all, like popping together a string of plastic pearls. My mother, full of reverence for me as long as I was adorable and simple, was too caught up in her own conditions. How could they respond to need when the children inside them had never grown up? Their attention was always focused inward, while they tried to finish the work of self-definition. It's all a gestation period. The artist might indirectly hope to one day "hatch" as an adult. They never do. If they did, their work would be finished.

Late last night at Jury's Inn, the bells came chiming in, bouncing from the walls and ceiling, jolting me awake. I had forgotten to close the window. Steve and Emmett were sleeping soundly. I lay there, just staring at the beige fabric walls, feeling anxious. I was unable to get a clear picture of us. Yes, we were going to try and find the castle and house, but what else was this trip supposed to be about? Though Dublin was just temporary, I felt bad about Emmett, having dragged him so far from home. I felt bad about Steve, who'd come because I'd asked him to. The creeping dark feeling that came over me had happened before. I was too far removed from all that was familiar. I missed home terribly.

For me, the players of this story weren't real, and by extension, we weren't either. My mother had been gone for *thirty-four years*, and too much time had gone by for my father. Why, especially at night, do the intimations of things, the sharp directives we have carved from obscurity, fall away? What right had I to drag Steve and Emmett all over Ireland looking for this elusive thing that neither of them could really understand? I wasn't that much different from my parents in some ways. After all, my own family were supposed to matter the most. What had I expected to find here? I watched them sleeping trustingly in this strange, hyped-up place with me, always with me, the bells shaking and clanging the hour outside our window.

A wave of terrible sadness and longing came over me, for Dad at home in New York. I picked up *Annaghkeen* and opened it to a few lines my mother had written about him on our last day on the island. We were going back and forth in the motorboat, packing up the VW with all of our things.

P, in his well-fitting suit rowed us across to the castle, where we secured the boat and transferred our belongings to the car.

In those few sentences about long ago, the scene filled in with the rapidity of spilled ink. It had been difficult to get along with him after my mother had died. He did not respond well to need. In some way we were always in opposition, though fond of each other at the same time, a strange and constant dichotomy. Since I had grown up and had my own family, I needed less from him, so we had a modicum of closeness. But my need of the old days was not gone and would never be gone. In Dublin, I felt a sick yearning, especially for him back *then*.

I ran my finger down the page, knowing exactly how he looked in his well-fitting suit. It would have been dark blue or charcoal gray or brown, of an expensive material, with slim lapels and a slim tie. It would have been cut like something out of a Fellini film. The suit straining a bit at the shoulders as he rowed, his brown curls combed close to his head and damp, his face morning pale and sharp as he checked things out around Lough Corrib. A marvelously handsome man. A keen blue eye that was always searching for the anomaly in nature, the fossil in the stone, the rare bird across the water. Sometimes warm blue eyes, ringed with crinkles. Eyes that survey the scene, and happening to find you in it, alight upon you with surprised amusement. Yes, you are still here, he is still here, he's thinking. If you say something funny, his laughter comes suddenly, with a jack-o'-lantern smile.

I shut the book, and the picture fragmented like blown ash. It had no solidity, no substance. It couldn't survive on its own but had to be summoned and embellished. It had to be *read*, powered by the reader's imagination. Like my mother, he was a literary creation. Once the covers were closed, he wasn't there.

In 1965, they each in their own way were at the starting point of becoming mythic figures. For once, I allowed myself the question of why life by itself could not be *enough*, why *we* could not. I wondered what I would have been *had* it been enough. I missed him, and my missing him was utterly useless. I knew he didn't miss me, not in the same way. Though he wanted me to be well, I was more an abstraction to him than a flesh-and-blood human being. I hurled *Annaghkeen* across the room, where it hit the desk facedown, slid over the faux wood surface, and crashed to the floor.

In the morning, we opened the window to see Dublin dressed in grays and browns with nary a hint of sun. Feeling worn out with gardens, grand houses, and abbeys, we decided to do something ordinary which would be good for Emmett too. We would give him time off from museums and tours and try to find a municipal pool. I called the front desk, and to my surprise they said, yes, there was one nearby where we could get passes for the day, and they had maps for us.

We did want to see the River Liffey and try to use it to orient ourselves. Once on the street, we were quickly surrounded by masses of sure-footed millennials, as it was rush hour. Weak rays of sun ventured through a break in the clouds, touching the buildings, the filigreed iron work, the polished and pert heads of the new professional class. A newspaper article I'd read at the hotel said that twenty-four percent of the population here was under twenty-five and had never seen hard times or even a mild recession. The new economy was fueled in part by their spending, and in Dublin, the energy was thick in the air. Stopping here and there to trace our route, we kept on and found a brown, watery expanse lined with buildings looking out: Essex and Wellington Quays.

Having just missed eight hundred years of oppression and poverty, young Ireland is well-educated and forward-looking. Maybe that legacy makes them especially strident and cheerful, happy to have been born when they were, wanting to get theirs while they can, as well as to make up for all the rest. Amid them and along the sides of the quays were a surprising number of homeless—a skinny, wild-haired teenager with teeth chattering in the sun, and kids sitting on the curbside among cigarette butts, as if daring cars to run over their feet. Here and there, a few crouched older people looked new to the streets and as wholesome as farmers, who they well might have been.

I might be resistant to too much largess because along with it comes rapid change. Perhaps, because of my history, I'm more comfortable when things don't move so fast. In our hometown of Sag Harbor, property values have skyrocketed. As I was growing up, our family doctor had his office in his house across the street from where I now live. They were there for forty years. When he died ten years ago, his house sold, and it has changed hands four times since then. It's where Alex and I had all our check-ups, and where my mother went with her first symptoms of cancer. It has turned from a holder of stories, or even a place to live (it is mainly unoccupied now) into a commodity. Though my cynical New York City side believes that everything unfortunately does have a price, markets on overdrive make that the dominant assumption, which causes great suffering. In Dublin, like any city, the main beneficiaries of prosperity are the strong and the sane, eddying around the less fortunate like water around shipwrecks.

On the street here, the casualties were vivid. One woman sat apple-cheeked among her multiple bags of possessions, a look of recent abandonment on her face. Had her family convinced her to sell her farm because prices were high? Was it a bad-seed kid? A pitiless husband with a booming business and a new wife? We gave the woman a few euros and went on, feeling lost ourselves. For Ireland, it has been a long, slow simmer. In poignant contrast to the current "boom" are the decades of preparation that led up to it. In the sixties, Ireland made a first-rate education available to anyone in the public schools, and so it offers an outstanding work force. The country pursued low-taxation policies to encourage companies, especially tech and finance, to relocate here. In 1973, Ireland joined the EU and was able to access Europe's large markets. There were changes in immigration policies and the breakup of the Soviet Union, all leading to massive inflows of foreign workers. Along the way, there were huge investments into public works, which are now paying off.

There are grumblers in Dublin and elsewhere. Those who believe that, in the race to embrace American-style capitalism, Ireland has lost something of its anagogic, nonmaterialistic self. And that very well might be true, at least in the big cities. Here was the exponential example, a shock wave of capital into a long-established, delicate structure. To keep pace with the world, a country must wrest a future out of the past, and it isn't often an ethical step forward, and even less a spiritual one.

Inside the pool building, we found a white-tiled reprieve. While we waited in line for our passes, the sounds of the street flipped on and off through the big double doors. There was the comforting but not-quite-the-same smell of chlorine and people coming by in shorts and tank tops with wet hair. In the pool were older people, families, a few college students doing laps, and a free swim area—great for Emmett and me. Fairly safe to say there were no tourists, though we didn't feel conspicuous at all. Steve pulled up a plastic chair and cracked the book he was reading. The water was warmish and stingy; we pulled on the little red-cloth bathing caps everyone must wear, our legs dangling in. Emmett looked happy as he slid into my arms, his small frame and back slippery with the odd cloudy chlorine, his legs wrapping around my waist. A nervous swimmer who also loves the water, he clung and peered over my shoulder.

Emmett's favorite thing to do, besides squirting water at me, is ride piggyback, getting teasingly close to the deep end. Emboldened, we then did his other favorite thing: he perches his feet on my shoulders, I spring up, and he goes flying. We did this at least ten times, his whoops reverberating around the white-tiled walls. Then he floated off on a kickboard to play on his own, leaving me with his unformed, fresh sense of things—the water's rustle, an echoing laugh, the slow unfurling walk of tired city people, young and sleek or old and crinkled, milk white, freckled, or fair, coffee-hued, wet hair under red caps, salt and pepper or luxuriant brown, some bathing suits new and bright, some saggy city-pool suits, puckered with a lack of elasticity.

I pulled my cap on tighter and went for a few laps. When I was done, I found that Emmett had made a friend, a little girl this time. They were having a joust with their kickboards. Then, outmanned, she got a weighted purple toy from her dad, and they took turns diving for it. She was as fast as a minnow, frequently getting the toy before Emmett did, and he obliged by not getting frustrated. Maybe that was because she was a girl. Usually, Emmett is quite competitive.

After a while, I sat out in the chairs with Steve and the girl's dad. His name was Matthew. Tall, brown hair, blue eyes that reminded me of Emmett's but for the color. Oddly, they were even more like my mother's eyes, azure, fringed with dark lashes. Eyes are usually distinctly feminine or masculine, but here they could have been either. His were dark-browed, with a look both far off and humorous at the same time. He had a quality of having been troubled considerably earlier in life and gotten himself in the clear.

In between the *hmmms* and *okays*, I could tell he thought our story fantastic and a little weird. Mercifully, he didn't have the stock response about how much Ireland has changed because he was from Canada and had not the history, having been here only five years. Hunkering down over his knees, his lingering and keen look upon the children seemed to exclude no possibilities, for them or for anyone.

He emphasized the luxury of our being able to drive almost the entire coast of Ireland; *that* was exciting, he said with a sort of guffaw. He wished he had the time. He loved Dublin, *loved it*, often flying over to Paris or London for the weekend. All this, for a boy from Ottawa. His house has quadrupled in value, and he just got tenure at Trinity College. A quick laugh added to his charm, that sense again of having gotten away from something obscure. Somehow, with his real estate and his plummy job, he wasn't quite finished with the escape. Steve wanted to know what his subject was. Philosophy, he said.

An hour later found us out on the street with our wet heads. It might've been odd for us to all go out for a drink. At least Steve wouldn't have been comfortable with it. He doesn't tolerate strangers well, except in the sort of fleeting instance that we had just had.

Matthew must have had this figured out. When he invited us out for a "quick beer," he appealed directly to me.

"What about the kids?" Steve immediately asked, not really wanting to go to a pub at any time, and if ever, just with us.

"We can bring them," said Matthew. "I know a family sort of place."

Olivia, the daughter, was playing imaginary jump rope, and Emmett was poking her with a pool noodle. Fixated on their important business, they were drifting away from us.

"Let's walk a bit," I said.

Matthew got out a packet of cigarettes. "I'd offer you one, but you Americans never smoke."

"I do. A little," I said. "Steve did for years and went cold turkey."

"Good for you, man!" said Matthew out of the side of his mouth while handing me one.

We went along, strolling in the evening warmth, watching the walking dance of the children up ahead, while they kept enough room between us to indulge in the fantasy of being on their own.

We found a park with a play area and sat for a long while. I asked Matthew about the homeless situation and all the revelers on the streets. He said it was no different now than when he first moved here. That was Dublin—rough, salty, ancient, and now electrified with cash. He looked around. His friendly consideration seemed to regard Dublin as a sort of oracle of the future. *His* future. He turned his face to me, considering me with black fringed eyes. I wondered about his open quality. In order to have a certain sort of oxygenated charm, it's helpful to be running from something. I poked and pried. There must've been a wife? But no, we weren't going to get on the subject of Ottawa, or way back then. It was all about right now and what we were doing, what we were about at the moment. I could hardly define it, and Steve began to regard Matthew with some wariness.

In between word tennis balls lobbed back and forth, Matthew's concentrated look appeared to say, *I knew you once, and after all, you've turned out pretty well.* The more meaningless the conversation became, the more and more this abstract idea took hold. We began to repeat ourselves, only going up to a certain point, filling in the rest with platitudes, while Steve looked uncomfortable. In retrospect, of course, I understood. We were only going up to a certain point, we all seemed to conclude at the same time.

We parted ways, saying goodbye to Matthew and Olivia. The children, as usual, were their casual selves. Okay, see you around, they seemed to say, in stark contrast to our ceremonious adieus, wishing each other well for the duration of life. Along with serious mileage between me and home, a series of fleeting meetings that color the space around me, have served to unload my closet of remorse, jammed as it is. Out goes the mournful face in the cracked frame. Out goes the box of broken toys. Out goes the chain mail suit. Out goes the beach scene and the empty, star-encrusted night, now dusty and flecked with mold—onto the rubbish pile. In the space of a few blessed minutes with a stranger, one gets the best self of the other, or even the spontaneous worst. It's all better than what one had before. In the closet, the floor is bare, a brilliant light falling through from the open door.

These are the uses of a city. With so much human experience tumbled together, it's possible that your own could not be all that different. It's possible to feel that fact seep into your body and mind and know, with hundreds of people brushing by, how little you matter. From there, it's not too far a jump to imagine the benefits of an anonymous tryst. You get the warmth, and each nameless kiss is touched with absurdity, canceling everything that went before it. You get to endanger your own reputation, heightening the eroticism (if you are that type). Because the meeting has no implicit meaning, you are allowed to inform it with a false one—intense, warm, winged. That is, if the spell is not broken.

Thus it was, I imagined, with the hen party group, that or some variation—though how could I know? The next day we saw them as we sat in the lobby in the enormous chairs with our coffees and Emmett's hot chocolate. They were checking out, some still wearing their ears, somewhat rumpled. Stacy, less effervescent now, fluttered her fingers at Emmett in greeting. The main difference between them and me was youth and freedom, though I saw myself still as young as they. Despite seeming settled, I always have difficulties catching up with the age I really am, perhaps because I didn't do these silly rituals.

The loiterers out front were the usual crew, mostly but not all male, bunching up in the early evening, watching people dragging cases and children, and men with overdressed women coming and going through the lobby, flicking their cigarette ashes around, hooting and hollering, tipping back their tall black cans. Their voices were hoarse and loud, without either the soft accent or tone of the country folk. Their laughter was contagious, echoing up and down the canyon between us and the cathedral, mixing at times with the bells. We wouldn't have gotten that at the Ritz, I told myself.

At about nine-fifteen, the floodlights went on, changing the cathedral from a monolith of staid and quiet granite to something much more active and alive. The crisp cutouts of the towers against the widening darkness were an invitation to its mysteries. It was designed this way to make people think about God. It just made me think about the sky and why the bums stand out there all day and all night. I kind of understood it. If I could stand not having a bed or much of a life, I might never go indoors.

I went down to the lobby to have a beer and make notes for the day, and heard the bells start up again through the window glass. It must have been some sort of a holiday because instead of the usual stop-and-start pattern, they were continual. So I crossed the street and walked around until I found a spot to stand and listen. A number of people, drunks yes, as well as tourists and families, were in the courtyard. There was a ruin of the first church that stood here, its ancient walls at knee-height in the green.

Standing there, the sound of the bells was so big I pictured it sweeping the outer edges of the city. The bells made me want to skip and dance and turn around in circles with my arms open wide and my face to the sky. I didn't, because I'm supposed to be grown up, and I am, for the most part, sober. I looked up to granite spires bathed in fluorescent frost, flat against a deep gray curtain, while the bells reverberated from the tower, reaching high and low, into the tired murky streets, over the heads of the young couple that sat necking, the drunks sitting in the ruin, the scurrying passersby, the towering buses and junky construction sites, overpriced pharmacies and bad Italian restaurants, pealing and tumbling down octaves at a time.

They stopped and then started again, so I ran back across the street to get Emmett and Steve. They got on their flip flops, and we went back over, dodging traffic. As soon as we reached the nearest church wall, the bells stopped. Steve joked that if we went back into the hotel, they would start again. He worried about the seedy types that were sitting in the ruin, while the bells began again, and the couple started kissing again, and Emmett began to run in circles around the ruin. I followed him, hopping through and around and on top of the old stones, on flying magic carpets of sound. Steve paced around, looking for the best acoustics, while Emmett and I ran, our steps landing in between each bang of the gong. Then Emmett was spinning, and I was spinning, my face to the gray sky, thinking, it's the same, the same. You've got to live every moment of life with all of your attention and stop wasting time being jealous of what might have been. In the church yard, I knew I was guilty of envy, not of someone else but of myself in some parallel existence. For a few moments, my envy fell away, and it was like being freed from weights I had been carrying around for years. All I could think of was how much the same it was. The bells going out, the same, the same, undulating around tree branches and shuddering the heads of birds, touching every steeple, every roof pinnacle, vibrating through every water tower, and tumbling down through alleyways and streets, into ears of every shape and size and color, reverberating and echoing the same the same the same.

Hoko Debby

This time the eighteen horsepower did not fail. We went north up the lake passing groups of islands arranged as though sprung up in the splash of a stone skipped from Galway to Cong. On one of them a thatched roof, twin-gabled house stamped a white place in a dense green hill. Huge trees bowered the surround and roughed an outline on the sky, but the house was open to the water. P gazed longingly. "That's just the right sized island. Wouldn't that be a great place to live?"

The passion of love is the passion of life unsatisfied by an object. There is something irretrievable and always missing, perhaps because it must always end. All joy wants eternity, deep, deep eternity.

A long with a good bit of remembering the post-Ireland years, Dublin was now in the dust. On our last day there, we had taken a taxi to the very house where the Braiders had lived, number one St. Helen's Road. As chronicled in *Annaghkeen*, the large brick house was the setting of the book's central lament, as my "then family" was falling apart. It was quite the same, though with a bigger garden than I remembered. From the sidewalk, I could see the living room window behind which all the drama had taken place. In 1965, we had been close to the end of our trip, just as Steve, Emmett, and I were now winding up ours. One St. Helen's Road was just another in a row of similar abodes, unremarkable, with prim, neat gardens on a street near the bay. I left, knowing I'd never return.

We had precise directions from the Jury's Inn staff, who often had to direct people to Cong. This time, no silent contemplations of the depths of Muckross Lake or the brown crawl of the Liffey. Our sightlines went out and were immediately sent back to us by asphalt and small towns, their buildings close to the road. Emmett slept in the back of the car, the stuffed snow leopard kitten that my father and Maria had given him pulled to his chest. Steve, directions in his hand, occasionally murmured about staying on track. "Don't worry . . ." the clerk at the Jury's Inn had said, ". . . couldn't be any easier." Huh, I thought, while having a sense of my own rickety present in high contrast to the events of 1970–1972.

Things had happened back then that felt separate from me, as love had become separate from me. Yet there was an odd familiarity to them, glaciers depth-fracturing hundreds of feet down beneath my feet. The surprises all came later, when how and where things had landed, and how permanent all of that was going to be, had sunk in.

A few years before I married Steve, I got a copy of my mother's death certificate and arranged for my father to sign a letter requesting her records from Sloan Kettering. I had looked at it only one time, stopped in my venture into the impossible by the top two documents—old-fashioned carbon copies of her heartbeat. The first one was from December 23, 1971, and the second one from January 13, 1972. These were electrocardiograms dredged up from a microfiche by someone in the records department. I pictured that person, whizzing by all the other reports and electrocardiogram printouts of people who had died that year—zeroing in on this small and ancient occurrence that had sent such severe repercussions through us for so long. I presumed the electrocardiograms were to demonstrate that in between those dates she was still living in her room, #M5, at Sloan Kettering hospital. The day that I looked at them, the shock was in the evidence of her life on paper, the particular peaks and valleys that were unique to her. Her heart had beat in this particular way, and for a long time. I had been close to it, I had heard it in my ear, I had felt its steady comfort. I had fallen asleep listening to its rhythm so many times. The printout was evidence of its end, and even after many years, the end was essentially unknowable. So I put it away.

Now, with Dublin behind us, I was brought up short to what I least wanted to consider—what I had avoided thinking about most of my adult life—the month, the day, the hour when something went horribly wrong in my mother's body, and she got sick.

In the summer of 1970, my father was working on *Blue Meridian*, and *Annaghkeen* had just been published. Alex was five, going to the Little Red Schoolhouse with the farm kids in our town. I was spending a lot of time with John and Dorothy Sherry and their three daughters, going to the experimental Hampton Day School and failing most of my classes. At home, the housekeepers came and went, and the parties churned on. Jackie Jackson, a babysitter who took care of us, remembered that after a big night my parents often wouldn't emerge from the bedroom until midday. Terry Southern, Cass Canfield Jr., Norman Mailer, Muriel Murphy, Lewis Lapham, and Merete Galesi were part of their close circle, as were Tom Guinzburg of the Viking Press and his wife Rusty, and my father's oldest friend, the landscape painter Sherry Lord and his wife Cile. My mother's brother, writer and journalist Kenny Love, and his family would sometimes visit, and they'd all shoot skeet in the backyard. Rip Torn, a friend of my mother's from her New York days, would visit. His name made me laugh. Was he serious?

When my father was home, especially in summer, our house was alight. I liked the atmosphere; I'd be allowed to stay only if I was quiet. I'd curl up on the sofa right in the middle of a raging cocktail party and read, my concentration perfect, as if the energy of the buzzing laughing people powered the story along. Reassured by the warm wafts of perfume, the smell of booze, and especially the exaggerated interest the revelers had in each other, I'd sink into a book better than any other place. Every once in a while, a heated face would poke into my sphere, "Whatcha reading? S'good?" A nice break. I'd tell them, chat, and they'd go away satisfied that they'd made contact with the child of the house, their guilt about leaving their own children at home assuaged. And always, somewhere in a sea of jeans, miniskirts, and pressed linen, at some point I'd spy the long tan legs of my mother and hear the particular whooping laugh that was hers and no one else's.

Sometimes, my mother would take me to New York on the train, and we'd stay at our apartment. These trips were always full of excitement. I loved the train; I loved New York, the pace of it and all the people. Once, we bought a Siamese kitten in a pet store near our apartment on the Upper East Side and brought it home in a cardboard box. I named it Sophia. My mother took me to see movies like *Carnal Knowledge* and *Five Easy Pieces* and would tell me who was stepping out on whom and who was the worst shit of all the characters, though she never said the word shit. She took me to a Noh play, and I slept through most of it. She took me around to see her friends on the East End of Long Island, John and Dorothy Sherry, Truman Capote and Jack Dunphy in their side-by-side houses near Sagaponack, Alfonso Ossorio and Ted Dragon in their art-filled fairyland "The Creeks" in East Hampton, and Muriel Murphy in her twin house in the Georgica Association. Muriel rented the unoccupied half to Lewis Lapham and Merete Galesi. My mother said that she loved it because she could see all her best friends in one stop.

Sometimes, late at night, she'd organize my room. I'd hear the shuffle of things and feel piles of clothes on my feet, comforted by the light and her near presence. She often didn't sleep well. I found among her mementos little pamphlets I had made for her called "The Sleeping Service." Inside, there was a place I would have her sign, on two separate lines, "Deborah" and then "Matthiessen," which I hoped would ensure her a good night's sleep. I worried about her; she seemed fragile to me. Often, she was away in New York teaching a course in Zen at the New School or on sesshins at Dai Bosatsu Zendo in the Catskills. When she was at home, sometimes we did Japanese tea ceremony. I was restless in the silence of tea ceremony but held out for the cookie, a white and green rice wafer with a coating of sugar on the back. At that time, she wanted me to be silent a lot. We were supposed to be concentrating on serious issues and centering ourselves. Whereas I was getting crushes on boys, worrying about how I'd look at a party. I developed a weird habit of walking with a lurching rocking step just to make my hair swing across my back. One day, she said, "Why are you walking like that?" I told her. She stopped me of the habit by saying, "If that's what it takes to make your hair swing, it's too high a price."

She did find this kind of thing funny, but not in a cruel way. Just the way life and all of its stages is funny. She'd look at me with a scientific eye, considering the phenomena of pubescent development with bemused detachment. I remember thinking that she was further down the line than me; everything had happened for her and to her in this way, and there wasn't a single ray of light in it. But it didn't have to be that way for me. Sometimes, she complimented me on the outfits I chose or said she wished her hair was as shiny as mine, always with a tinge of sadness, as if it didn't really matter how shiny it was. If I had romantic hopes, I was in for a lot of disappointment.

One time, we went to Bloomingdale's in the city, and I wanted a hot-pink shift with fluorescent-green trim. I loved the dress and had little hope when I asked for it because we never bought many things except at the beginning of the school year, and it was too flashy anyway. I was astonished when she bought it for me. I felt as though it was for me and me only because she didn't like the dress or even the idea of the dress. I was thrilled.

I don't think my parents had any idea why I wanted to go to England to boarding school. About a year before I had the idea, my mother sat me down one day, wanting to talk. I immediately said, "You want to send me to a shrink." She was startled that I had guessed so fast. I'm glad she thought of it. I had a wonderful therapist, Miriam McKenzie, who was fond of me and I her. I saw her on and off for years, and after my mother died. That I was gaining weight was noted and addressed with a restriction on after-school cookies. That I was unhappy was noted, and the therapist called up. It is perhaps unrealistic to compare one's own childhood to the way one treats their own child. Still, I never felt looked after the way I look after Emmett in the day to day. I never felt like the changing, evolving being that I must have been at twelve. I rarely felt *visible* except when I was funny. I felt heavy, ugly, chipped out of granite, my entire being going numb, and my face turning to stone, which is why I was desperate to leave.

In Sagaponack, an older girl, about sixteen, whom I had a bit of a crush on, was going to a school in England called Cobham Hall. That summer, she gave me the number and said to call them, that I could probably get in. So I did call late one night while my parents were out. I was accepted over the phone. When they came home that night, I asked them if I could go, and the next day they said yes. I had no idea what I was getting myself into. Neither one of them asked me one question about it. Cobham Hall in England was just another piece of an ongoing puzzle falling into place. I didn't feel sorry about leaving my mother because she was suffocating me. I didn't feel sorry about my father because I thought that he didn't really want me around, that if given the choice between me being there or not, he would have chosen the latter. He was involved with Alex, not me. I was just going to have to go.

That summer, my mother helped me to get ready, assembling the clothes I would need, arranging to hire the international nanny that would meet me at Heathrow and take me to Harrods for the uniform. I was in her room, and she had just gotten out of the shower. She was looking in the mirror. Her belly was distended; she was mystified. "I'm not due for my period," she said. Because of her allergies, she had always been a bit of a hypochondriac, peering intently at moles, patches of eczema, and any changes in her skin. She went to the doctor often. I didn't think of it again.

While leaving for the airport, my mother was crying outside her bedroom door. Her eyes were wet, which astonished me. She was very tender and so forlorn. At twelve, I hadn't a real concept of how far away I would be. I was just following an idea. Somehow, in its execution it had become serious and sad. We had a long hug. I felt as though I was leaving a child behind. Now, to think that just then she was being diagnosed with the disease that would take her life is heartbreaking to me. I can't imagine having to say goodbye to Emmett in a similar situation. Yet it was part of a strange continuity—the tenor of the years before this, the endings that *Annaghkeen* had foretold.

Through talking to my father and the Sloan Kettering report, I found that she had had a hysterectomy that fall. When she recovered, they went to ski in the French Alps and came to England to see me at Cobham and take me out to lunch. My English schoolmates were astonished by the glamour my parents threw off as they walked from their car to the front hall to fetch me. I remember crowding into the window together, watching them come across the wide lawn, my father in a gray suit, my mother in a wrap dress and heels, her dark hair soft about her face, her eyes a luminous blue. I was so happy to see them. One mean girl—skinny, pretty Carol with tousled brown curls—said, "Those are your *parents?*" while the others just stared and then looked at me in disbelief.

At the lunch, my mother complained about my clothes. My dress was held together with safety pins in places where it was coming apart. She wondered why the school wouldn't have seen to it that I was properly dressed. Of course, we didn't have that kind of oversight there, and we were in uniform most of the time. We didn't talk about her illness. I was in no way aware of it. By that time, I was quite homesick; the school was rough for me. I wasn't good at making friends, though I had a few. There was quite a lot of anti-American sentiment among the girls.

Come summer, I was back at home, and they were hoping that the hysterectomy had been a success. I knew none of this. I was thirteen, spending most of my time at the Sherrys, starting to smoke pot and becoming close with a troubled girl who was going to another boarding school in the U.S., North Country in Lake Placid. Midway through the summer, I announced that I wanted to go there. My parents said, okay, again without asking me anything about what I was thinking or what the school was like. They seemed to have no plan, just driving blind, letting me do whatever I wanted. This is understandable considering what they were going through, though I knew nothing about it at the time.

In the fall of 1971, my mother had symptoms again. According to my father, at about that time she discovered some nodules and went to see our family doctor, Robert Semlear in Sag Harbor, to have them biopsied. He had been a friend and tennis partner over the years, and I remember he had a good bedside manner. I'm sure it was with great care and gentleness that he called them in to let them know the results they feared. The "Summary of Management" page from the Sloan Kettering microfiche said, "about four months prior to admission she was seen again on Long Island, where she had a subcutaneous nodule biopsy which was confirmed showing adenocarcinoma." I was at my new school in upstate New York, a five-hour drive north, screwing up, failing everything, hanging out with the rebels. I knew none of it, and when the time came that it was absolutely clear, I refused to see it. The cancer had returned, and her chances against it were slim.

My mother's friend Merete was another who followed her into Zen. She told me that Deborah had said more than once that she would do almost anything to keep her marriage together, and that after two previous tries, she absolutely had to make it work.

By the late sixties, my parents were entrenched in battle with themselves and each other. The conundrum seemed to be that of living, breathing, and dying, as much as it was their marriage. From early on, they talked about death, almost as if talking about it, writing about it, and thinking about it could solve it. After we moved over to my father's house near the sea, there soon appeared a real human skull that he had picked up on one of his expeditions. Somehow, it ended up in my mother's study, propped on a low bookshelf behind the fireplace of white-painted brick. Its eyes were green coins of an abalone-like material that caught the light when you went past. Its jaw was wired with flat twine. I only went past it a few times and avoided it at all costs. Its presence was palpable to me. It was terrifying. I thought about it all the time, glomming into the dark or the day, watching, pulling at us somehow. It had once belonged to a person, *been a person*, and now that person had taken up residence in our house. But I knew why it was there.

Along with other morbid preoccupations, my mother and father each claimed that they weren't going to live past forty. And then when they passed forty, they still said, standing around the kitchen island of a winter afternoon, "It will be me," and then the other, "Nope, it will be me. You'll see." Their humor was black, a cheerful dare, as if they could face death down by living with it every day. They were like two kids peering over the edge of a high cliff, only the children would have seen how far a drop it was and found some other way to play. Not Deborah and Peter. The skull, along with a shrunken head from New Guinea that my father kept in his studio, were there as reminders. Beneath it all, the jest was serious, and wearying the despair that ran through it. The separating-in-Dublin chapter of *Annaghkeen* replayed over and over again—my father unable to resist temptation, my mother trying to survive the roller coaster of his affairs, her own moods, and the criteria that she had set for herself, "this time," in order to save the marriage. I believe that as a consequence, a chasm opened up. Then there was room between them for a major, life-altering event. There was room for something catastrophic that might be redeeming, that might open the door to the wisdom they were looking for. The discovery of a malignancy in 1971 seemed to have been as she had written it a few years before in *Annaghkeen*.

Thanksgiving break I was home from school in Lake Placid, thirteen, and innocent of all. In the morning, my mother worked at her desk upstairs. By the afternoon she was in bed most days because of the pain. Instead of hiring a nurse, I was nominated to take care of her. I was to make her the things she could eat: a light custard called flan and Cream of Wheat. Later, my father told me the decision to have me help was an effort to get me to acknowledge what was happening. I spent hours sitting with her on the bed as she writhed in pain. I was absolutely unmoved. I refused to comprehend; I couldn't jump out of myself and start to think about her, about what it might be that I was seeing. My job was to make the food and call my father in from the studio if it got too bad. And so I did all of that, somewhat mechanically. That this was a grave situation never occurred to me at any time. I remember creeping through every movement, doing what was asked. But it was as if I was no longer in the building. One afternoon, while I was sitting there, likely with my face set in stone, she went through a bout of horrible pain, moaning and crying out. She looked at me angrily and said, "Why are you so passive?" I couldn't answer her. I didn't know why I was, though I felt bad about it and sorry for her. I never knew at any point what was being asked of me. Had I known, I was sure, somewhere deep inside myself, that I would not be up to the task.

I went back to the school in upstate New York. During the Christmas break, I stayed with my Uncle Kenny in the city and came to see my darling Mama at Sloan Kettering, in room #M5. She had a private room with a window to look out of. She was propped up in bed, smiling, with one of the bed jackets she liked to wear over her nightgown. She was frail and luminous, her eyes much bigger than usual. She seemed very happy to see me. I had made her a blue tea ceremony bowl for Christmas in my ceramics class at school. When I gave it to her, she was so delighted. She was absolutely radiant with love, holding the bowl like it was the most precious thing she'd ever had. The atmosphere in the hospital room was reverential, waiting, and quiet. The solemnity surrounding us there had the same quality as the zendo at home and the Zen Studies Society in the city where she had taken me so many times. The mood was one of cessation. It had a directive, which was that everything stop, and that everyone, especially me, be silent and full of veneration and stillness. The hospital was just more Zen. As I had before, I became that tranquil, halted person for the sake of my mother, though it wasn't natural to me. I knew that it was even more important in the hospital, though I didn't dare ask why. I tuned out the whole picture and took only what I could stand, that I was happy to have hugged her and made her happy with my gift of the bowl, believing that she was just especially emotional that afternoon, not feeling well, and nothing else was wrong.

I went back up to school. Three weeks passed, and I then had a call from my father. It was arranged for me to take the call in the science room in the basement, as there were no phones in the dorms. Light from either the moon or streetlamps fell through the high half-windows, illuminating the toads and turtles and displays of beetles under glass. I will never forget that room. The day's lesson was still on the blackboard. My father, sounding far away, was calling to tell me that Mom was "very sick." I asked him, "Could she die?" And he said, yes, she could. I cried on the phone with him. He would not move from his words, he would not, he could not soften them. *Yes, she could die* rang in my ears for days. I was very sad, I was frantic. I felt absolutely powerless.

A week passed. While in the dorm, I got a letter from her sister, Cynthia (Muffin) Love. It was short and said, "We will all be missing your mother." I got upset again, and the dorm mother and father were not there. But there was an older girl who lived there, an assistant named Becky from the town. She had long, brown-blonde hair, and was tall and thin. She came to my room to tell me that she was very sorry to say that my mother had died. She was sweet and sad. I was beside myself, wondering why all of this was going on without me. Still, at the time, I didn't know the extent of death. I had no idea how wide, how deep, how long it was.

My father came to the school a few days later to pick me up for a family trip to his parents' house on Captiva Island in Florida. It was early February 1972, a blizzard. The drive took all day, a gray metallic light inside and outside the car. My father had to drive very slowly to stay on the road. I don't remember that we spoke much.

Perfect opposites, inseparable in their separateness, they embody a paradox, alone in which is found the whole.

After she died, on more than one occasion my father told me that all of the strife, the arguments over petty things, all the poison and resentments fell away after she had become seriously ill. He described in particular walking with her on the beach after they had gotten the results from Dr. Semlear's biopsy. The two cried together, my father with her in a way that he had not been for years. He made a point of it, and his words had a note of penitence that was for me alone.

While she was ill, aside from the pain, my mother was often vividly happy. When I had to call my father in from the studio, I remember her relief at seeing him walk into the bedroom. I remember his presence in the hospital room, his gentle oversight. She needed him, and *this* time he came through. He was absolutely present for her illness, loving and concerned with her comfort and care, to the point where she referred to him as "St. Peter" to her friends. After years of spiritual aspirations and disappointments, my mother was still imbued with a romantic ideal of *perfect opposites, inseparable in their separateness.* Mercifully, she would have someone there, someone really with her, and it turned out to be the man she loved. I think that was a great deal more comforting to her then a stack of books and cryptic Zen koans.

On my father's part, he embellished on the story of the beach walk to say that from that day until she died was the most romantic time he had ever had with anyone. He added that "of course" they could not be physical, but still, he said, they were very much in love.

At thirteen, this statement was completely unmanageable. *Why did you wait so long?* I inwardly wailed, wishing that he could have managed something better while she was well. I remember not understanding it. She had been the same person when she was well; she didn't transform into *someone else* with the advent of sickness, someone different and more lovable. She was the same, just sick. Besides being full of grief and the slow-blooming realization that I would never see her again, the years after she died were completely confusing to me.

At the memorial service at the Zen Studies Society, I was praised by one of the Zen masters in his speech as having "dignity." I remember thinking that this was absurd. I was not dignified; I was frozen and numb. They were mourning, and what had happened to me was so unfathomable I couldn't even feel it. At the least, nothing about it was going to be contained or assuaged in the slightest way with gongs, chants, and bits of poems. They were well-meaning people who tried to help me, and they looked and sounded as if they were behind a wall of glass.

A few months went by, enough time to send an echo back from where my mother had once been: in her study with her stacks of books, in the Zendo breathing quietly, in my mind, in all of our minds. In that sad wake came a lot of women stopping by, doing my laundry for mysterious reasons, showing up with casseroles and hopeful smiles. I don't remember that I felt obligated to be polite the way I would now to people trying to help, even with their own agendas ticking away behind their eyes. Being left to find one's own way has its benefits. Despite troubles in our family, I had never been pressured to "be nice," which I appreciate because to make that effort would have separated me from myself further than I already was. Soon I was back up at school.

At the end of the term, my father came to pick me up. This time, on the long drive down, he told me that my biological father, Clement Pollock, had died in Mexico. He was forty-six. I remember the news bouncing off me with barely a vibration. It was a footnote to the new way I always felt, completely adrift and tethered to no one except Alex and a few friends and, in a remote sort of way, my father, Peter. Pollock wasn't liked in our house, and I had few real memories of him. Later, I was sorry that he had died because his death was a waste and mostly his own fault, as he had been slowly killing himself with booze since his youth. I was especially sorry that I wouldn't be able to knock on his door one day, just for the hell of it. He would have had to let me in.

When I came home for summer, I found that Alex had suffered at his school where the kids razzed him about his "dead mother," which made me furious. Alex, turning eight, looked small and vulnerable to me. I remember wanting to clock the idiots at his school, to fix him up somehow, and take away that miserable loss that had happened to him. We became very close, wrapped around each other watching TV or reading. Much later, Alex told me that as he got older, he felt sorry for me because Pollock was gone too. We helped each other through, even though he was younger than me by six years. More than ever, he was one of the few bright spots I had.

After my mother was gone, her siblings Mary, Cynthia, and Nathalie were not included much in my father's life. Kenny Love was an exception—he and my mother had broken off from the original St. Louis gang with what my Aunt Mary had called "worldly aspirations" and come east. Kenny had been alongside my father at the hospital, and he was part of literary circles on the East End of Long Island, so they still knew each other. In Sagaponack, people came and went, mostly literary people and the people who followed them. There were quite a few outrageous parties, girlfriends coming and going, top models, art world people, and more LSD. Some, a few, had a little interest or time for children. There was no kindly, slow, observant, constant sort of person around except my therapist,

Miriam Mackenzie in East Hampton. My sister Jessie Pollock (Clement Pollock's older daughter), an artist ten years older than me, lived in Philadelphia. My father had a soft spot in his heart for her and a deep respect for her work. John Sherry and his family remained good friends with my father and included me in their fun, rough-and-tumble world for years. But these few comfortable souls were not very much a part of the immediate stratosphere at my father's house. In Sagaponack, things were cold. I was associated with the departed era, and I felt my lack of relevance before the last sighing chant of the Kannon Sutra rang out.

The summer of 1972 was one of the oddest and most memorable of my life. I was caught between missing my mother and trying to cordon off her memory. He *was* famous now, she *was* gone, and much had changed, much more than I ever could have conceived of. Our lives were turned inside out, and chairs for the spectators were assembled—not by us—on the lawn. It was a packed house. In between scenes, the audience opined: When my mother married my father, he had a lot of promise but hadn't yet had a big success. She hadn't fulfilled her housewifely duties and so suffered the consequences when he strayed. My father was a certain "sort of man," who would outgrow her. It was okay to have ambitions, but she took it too far. He couldn't deal with kids; he just wasn't that type. My mother could have done more; she could have made him happy. My mother had Alex to try to save the marriage, and it hadn't worked. Following that failure, the only way she was going to remain with Peter was to perish and provide him with a tragedy that he could write about. They never said this within earshot of my father, but it was bandied about for quite a while.

Another theory floated around, which handily fit in with the overall picture. My mother was sad, cried more than was normal, and so perhaps it was for the better that she was gone from this world. They said this where I could hear. Some said it right to me. It was the seventies, after all. Children were considered to be just smaller versions of grown-ups, and truths, even just speculative ones, were considered always beautiful and worth hearing. I remember their hard, calculating faces and watching them wonder about me. From their accumulated experience, they cast out scenarios like fishing lines, trying to hook not only what had happened but what was going to happen. Much of it was incredibly bizarre. It had an ugly shape, a muddy and dark cloud on the horizon, a monster blown across the sea to hover over the water down the road from our house. I might have to deal with something similar, I thought, but it would be much later, when I was older. Meanwhile, I would protect myself. I would be blind; I would be deaf. Their opinions were not my concern. They had nothing to do with me or, essentially, my mother. I knew the child-like Deborah that lived inside the adult she was, that corresponded so well with the child I was and that needed protecting. That was windblown and sad. I missed her terribly. The only good thing about her being gone was that she wouldn't ever have to hear any of the things they said.

Much, much later, I was able to look back dispassionately and see what had happened. People were coping with catastrophe by turning it into fodder to support their own views. Like a stream driven from its source, the accepted logic was turning and twisting to fit around the tragedy. At thirteen, I wasn't capable of applying significance or creating stories to tell myself or anyone else. I had no outlook at all. It was as if an entire world had fallen away and a chasm opened up where my mother had been. I could have been standing in midair. I did say to my brother Luke, "Maybe we'll all get along better with each other now." He had praise for my words, and I don't even know why I said them. Did I really think it was true? Or was I just doing what everyone else was doing, coming up with my own brand of bandage?

What I did later come to understand is that people always want a symbolic culmination of the story. They look for meaning—in life, in death, doesn't matter. Pieces will be rearranged. Lines between truth and myth will blur. What they want is the whole, and a couple make the whole. My mother wanted it, my father wanted it, and I wanted it (but with my mother *alive*). Had Alex been asked, he would certainly have said that he wanted Mommy and Daddy to always be together.

A year went by. The summer of 1973, my father began preparing for a three-month long expedition. He would join biologist George Schaller, walking west under Annapurna and along the Kali Gandaki River, 250 miles to the Tibetan Plateau. Schaller wanted to study the bharal, or Himalayan blue sheep, and my father was interested in the Himalayan snow leopard that would likely be hunting the sheep while they were congregated in rut. At that time, Schaller knew of only two Westerners, himself being one, who had seen the snow leopard in twenty-five years, which made the hunt for a sighting all the more intriguing.

In Sagaponack, my father bought hiking boots and went for a long walk on the beach every day in order to break them in. He would tell me again about the months leading up to my mother's death, the walk on the beach, the permanent collapse of the wall of troubles between them because he was shaping a narrative of his own. Very much in my mind was still the question, *Why did you wait so long?* I thought that one day I might talk to him honestly and get him to explain it. But he was so unpredictable. He had to be in a certain sort of rare mood for these kinds of conversations and initiate them himself. And there had to be time. There wasn't any because he was remote and consumed with his panacea: work. Specifically, he was taken up with the preparations to go away for a long time on the snow leopard expedition.

As my family and I spun down the M6 toward Cong, looking for my past (and ostensibly, theirs), I wondered, who owns the memory of someone? Who shapes a personality of the past? Who decides? Will it be one or two, or thousands? Will it be three or four, or multitudes? Does what they were go on in the thoughts of someone who'd needed them, in the sharp shock of a thing they would have laughed at, the stranger passing by who has the same look about the eyes, or a scrap of a song they loved? Or are they more alive as a collective perception in the minds of many—in a famous painting, or in a piece of writing, at the moment when the portrait is complete or the reader is transported? Is that more valid? More real? Does a big audience make it more valid? Is it more valid when multiplied by fame?

In 1972, it was as if Deborah herself, the former flesh and blood Deborah, was being eased down a ladder into the abyss to suit a cornucopia of ideas. Unfulfilled romance (*love's most complex form*), spiritual longing, the existential adventurer made even more brave by dying young, and herself as a sort of saint. John Sherry said that she had "no mud on her soul." My father wrote of Deborah in *The Snow Leopard* as having at times an "above-life quality as if she were practicing for the day when the higher state that she aspired to must come." He depicts her as hard to live with because "saintlike aspiration presents problems." He fleshes out his portrait without putting her on a pedestal, which she would have abhorred. However, for all the truth telling, a reverse magic happens—she is mythologized, and especially her death is mythologized. Through it, in *The Snow Leopard*, my father experiences and encounters his own mortality with great beauty and poignancy, in much the same way she encountered the end of love in *Annaghkeen*, all intertwined with *her* mortality. In *Annaghkeen*, she seeks to solve her need for him with a spiritual understanding and feels her encroaching death through the death of love, while in *The Snow Leopard* he rubs shoulders with eternity (something he has always longed to do) through the catastrophe of her death. Much of what he learned from Deborah, ways that he sees the world in this deep and soul-searching memoir, are a result of her influence. During his trek into Asia, he seals his commitment to Buddhism, as she shows him from beyond the grave how to heal himself from her loss. The two books are mirror images of each other. *The Snow Leopard* is his *Annaghkeen*, for he never wrote another book remotely like it. Now they are side by side on my shelf, twinned in art, impossible in life. (I must qualify here that I don't think the responsibility of art is to be like life. Art has its own atmosphere.)

The Snow Leopard went on to win the National Book Award twice ('79 and '80), in two categories. It is his most successful book, having sold into the hundreds of thousands and been printed (legally) in twenty-five to thirty languages. It is on numerous venerated travel book lists and is used in school and college curriculums in the U.S. and abroad. You can buy a bootlegged version of it on the street in Kathmandu for ten dollars, the cover a monochrome reproduction and the type fat and blurred from a worn-down press. On almost every trek into the mountains of Nepal and Tibet, at least one person is reading it and loving it. It is alive. It is my father, at his most stripped down and revealed. It has the tender side of him, which not many get to see. It has all the best of him, the best that my mother inspired.

So the wagging tongues weren't altogether wrong. In *The Snow Leopard*, Deborah and Peter *were* finally made whole, their union blessed for eternity, if only in the minds of the reading public (which in literary circles is often the most important thing). This was the world with which we were surrounded— permeated with the love of stories and literature, the love of writers and poets, the romantic, needful gestalt of a community and a greater reading public who thought of themselves too as grainy figures walking on the beach, absorbing some great and tragic news, the key to eternity held loosely in their hand. The day is cloudy but not rainy. The picture is black and white. The walkers are tall and photogenic, at the peak of their attractiveness. It isn't insignificant that they are stunning, and one would always stay that way. Or that one's death would illuminate the other, culminating in spiritual understanding in a work of great beauty. This is where he can meet her, where they can finally be together. From start to tragic end, any reader can take this into themselves and become wiser too, perhaps even by becoming a Buddhist. Deborah, shaken out and revamped, can give them back themselves in legendary form, endowing their lives with significance. They needed her, oh they needed her, and she provided, and so did we.

Deborah—"exceptionally intelligent and kind," my father wrote. "The tender one," John Love, her father, called her. So honest, so youthful. So tragic. Too innocent and gentle for this world, many people said. Not tough enough, my father often said. "As beautiful and sad as Éire itself," wrote Nancy Wilson Ross about *Annaghkeen*. "Too intelligent for her own good," said my sister Jessie. "Hoko Debby," Zen master Eido Shimano

Rōshi named her. A romantic, a "man's woman," said many others. "No mud on her soul . . ." Eccentric, troubled, sad, restless Deborah. Existentially brave—a pioneer. A femme fatale, a charmer, a star. Always beautiful, never to be old. Never to wrinkle and fade away. A future between the covers of a best-selling book would have been more appealing to her than the Real Life she had.

Funny Deborah, with a necklace hanging from her long knobby nose while pretending to dust the house. Who said silly things like, "Take it easy, greasy. You've got a long way to slide." Who couldn't cook worth a damn. Who published the journals I wrote in a composition book that summer in *Annaghkeen* as an important part of the whole story of us. Whose little smile hovering at the corners of her mouth let us know that we were good from the tops of our heads to the tips of our toes. Deborah, just a mom—perhaps the least interesting part to anyone, but vitally important. Leaving two children behind.

She wouldn't have minded how it all turned out. In fact, she might've been thrilled. Though she might well have wondered, as I certainly have, at what it took.

Old Timers

Daisies flew among the white butterflies; yellow loose-strife and brown-rayed knapweed bounded about the meadow; a wren flitted in the thorn hedge behind me. I ate Caerphilly cheese and bread and after took Yeats from the basket, but I could not read for looking, and could not look for thinking; could only finally sink back into the grass and close my eyes.

Entering a small wood we came upon a sixteenth-century ruin, a vast area of roofless walls beside the Cong River. Green flat-bladed weeds flowed in undulations from their anchorage beneath the brown crystalline water, and the river seems a piece of faultless amber holding the ancient flora of a million years.

We are on our way to Annaghkeen Castle. On the "carriage-way" this morning, while going under a weird white overpass of obscure purpose, the pith of that one short summer jumped out at me. It wasn't an obvious place to remember anything; there was no foreshadowing of such a recollection. On one side, supported by stacks of painted white cinder block, the overpass looked more like an East German bulwark than anything Ireland could have constructed. It certainly hadn't the romance that would've caught my mother's eye.

We zipped under it, cutting through the bumpy grassy hills, while I knew in an instant that I had seen it before, and at the time, there had been a lot going on. I was taking stock, as much as a seven-year-old can. I had no plan, no design, wanted no particular result. I had no desires beyond (had the question been asked) staying with the pack and the pack staying together: Alex at home to be returned to at the summer's end, and Mom, Dad, and Luke in the car.

In those few seconds between the approach to this conglomeration of pipe cleaners and cinder block and leaving it behind, my understanding, up to then having slowly expanded in minuscule and invisible ways, made a leap into the future, into the wide white morning sky. On that day, in what had been a unified, somewhat predictable world, fissures appeared. The whole thing went a little to pieces. Along with the new awareness, the people in the car became stranger. My mother was in front, her bobbed black hair streaked with gray, her triangular knees pushed up against the glove compartment, her long, elegant hands wrapped around her brown spiral notebook. Lukie was with me in the back seat, his sharp features still soft with baby fat, scowling a warning at me to keep back. Dad was at the wheel, a road map on his knees, peering at each road sign we passed. All of us close enough to feel each other's breath.

I found myself for the first time a thing apart from them, and they were all separate from each other. And separate from the streak of green by the roadside, the high white sky, and the undulating, stony hills beyond. This was not entirely bad. To be a mere brushstroke in a painting or a note in a song is too much a part of the whole to have any power. And at seven, I naturally wanted power. At that moment, I began to know that in order to have any effect one has to choose and become separate. At first, the separation looks like nothing so much as a door cracked open to a larger room—another space in a long continuum of spaces that one has gone in and out of over and over forever. Out of curiosity, a foot jams into the door and begins to pry it open. At the time, one has no idea how enormous the room is—what is this new place? A place of pieces, a giant jigsaw puzzle. It takes years and years to find out that its contents are terrifying, and that once through, there's no walking back through the door.

On the carriageway, there was a glimmer of the old intelligence. This didn't have anything to do with the original travelers, or even the current ones. It was only a way of inhabiting the world—a faint reed of a suggestion of what had come before the door. What had it been? There weren't any words for it.

Emmett didn't care a bit about anything I'd been thinking, or the way the countryside was changing, or how he himself was changing. Surrounded by his books and toys in the back seat, he was rapt in a world of his own. We prompted him from time to time to look out of the window and notice at least that we had left the Dublin suburbs far behind. That we were crossing the bottommost sliver of Mayo County on our way to a magical village called Cong.

Around us the grid of short stone walls divided the fields, with a verdant green between them and the occasional nodding, old-growth tree. Like *Annaghkeen* accounts, this countryside had more animals than people: black-and-white cattle, black and black-and-white sheepdogs, little runty brown dogs, the occasional donkey or skinny cat, a herd of sheep huddled in a corner of a field. Sometimes a farmer, walking around his barn. Along the road, the land rose and fell, and on a rise there was usually a house. The plots were generally large, and vegetation kept to a minimum, so there was an opportunity to see past the house to a patchwork field, and another, and another, with bright open air stretching out over the land.

In addition to the disappearance of the sweet thatch-roofed cottages I remember, there was a strange phenomenon we had seen on our travels, that of the old cottage or homestead left on the same plot. Sometimes you see two dwellings, the bigger one a new bungalow-style house with staring picture windows and asphalt driveway. These new places are short on adornment. If we had a house with soil and precipitation like Ireland has, there would be no end to the plants—all tangled roses and blooms and walkways with ivy-covered trees. The preference seemed to be for short-clipped lawns, one or two small ornamental bushes, and perhaps some evergreen beds along the house itself. Not more than two or three extra things. But in some cases, another extra thing quite nearby. The old family homestead. A third to a half smaller than the new place, made of stone and white plaster, and possibly degraded thatch, usually not maintained. The old grandparents' place, empty-windowed, blasted by the elements, looking upon the sparkling existence of the descendants. Does it sharpen the relish of the new generation? Is it a way of not forgetting when the family was poor? Is it an attempt to say, yes, we were humble then, and we aren't going to get too far from it no matter how well we're living? Knowing Steve and his family as well as I do, I thought it was the latter.

From the road, I imagined I smelled the water of Lough Corrib. On R334, we were alongside it for a long while, forty miles of it, though at too much of a remove to be able to see it. On the map, the place names we went through were cryptic, and none had I heard of before or read noted in *Annaghkeen*. Steve read them out as best he could: Ballisnahyny, Bunnafollistran, Torbernaderry. Nowhere was there a sign for Annaghkeen, while around us the countryside began to look familiar, more so than any other I'd seen. Hanging in the air between Steve and me was a new plural aspect of this venture. I had thought of it privately many times, while he, in Ireland for the first time, had been taken up with first impressions of the country. The novelty having worn off, we silently faced the question together—how much would remain here? After all, it was just another place.

Cong is a pretty town. One encounters wide, shallow streams at almost every corner of this ancient enclave, shagged at the banks with purple melic grass and floating sweetgrass in the current. Since my mother didn't emphasize it, I wasn't prepared for the way the village is encircled with water (there are four bridges) or the dollhouse side streets with tiny houses trimmed in bright salmon and azure hues. Still, for being geared to tourists, Cong could not be called garish. Not one tchotchke emporium, not one leprechaun with a hangover. A beautiful ruin sits at the center, Cong Abbey, which my mother did write about toward the end of *Annaghkeen*, her imagination captured by the grace of its floral capitals and Romanesque doors.

We found our inn across from the Cong River. While the proprietress was opening up the rooms, I asked if she had heard of Annaghkeen Castle. She had not. When I mentioned the dates, she said there was an old-timer around Cong we could talk to, and she mentioned another old guy who hung around Ashford Castle. All these old-timers, I thought. Are we that old? Is it really that late? Steve asked how old the old-timer at the castle was, perhaps wondering the same thing. In his seventies, she said. She was probably in her mid-thirties, born when we were in high school. In order to explain her lack of knowledge about Annaghkeen Castle, she said that she was from "twelve miles away" and looked sort of helpless.

She suggested that we go to the tourist center to see about local maps. "You'll find there are many castle ruins on the Corrib," she said, as if one would do as well as another. When she spoke the whole name of Lough Corrib, the "g" and the "h" were almost silent, and "Corrib" sounded like "Chaarrib . . ." which had a soft, magical sound. Almost worth crossing the ocean for alone. I hadn't heard it pronounced that way, or any way at all, for such a long time. At the same time, I was beginning to think it wise to scale down expectations. Whether we found Annagh-keen or didn't, our conversation with her emphasized, as so many do, the staggering amount of time that had gone by.

Nearly a *half century*.

The term bounced around in my head while unpacking sweaters, books, socks. Across from the inn, the merry jingle of the Cong River wound around the dreaded chunk of time. A *tenth* of five hundred years. What was going on five hundred years ago in Cong? While Steve and Emmett poked around the restaurant downstairs, I consulted a few tomes I had brought with me, chief among them the definitive account of this region, still widely read, *Wilde's Lough Corrib*, by Sir William Wilde (1815-1876), Oscar's father. He was a Dublin surgeon and an antiquarian, with a country house very near Cong.

I have difficulties with facts, especially historical ones. And there we were, in another place soaked with antiquity and old stories. If present-day Cong were the nose of a comet, its white blazing tail would slice the sky in half. There was Ashford Castle (current incarnation: 1868) and the much earlier Cong Abbey, circa 1128.[10] Though Ireland was ruled by regional kings for centuries after, the last *High King* of all of Ireland, Roderic O'Connor, lived out his days in the Abbey after he was deposed in 1191.[11] The problem is that I don't really believe these things. Until I believe them, I can't remember them. I must first humanize them, cut them down to size and acclimate to them before I can consider them real. So I would read up on it first and tell Steve. He loves data of all kinds, especially nugget-sized bits that he can put into his trove of information.

The year in question, 1506, five hundred years ago. My time away from Cong approximately times ten. Beyond the brochure I had, I could find only a smidgeon about Cong proper because record keeping did not commence here until 1870. William Wilde wrote, "To follow out the history or annals of Cong in succession during the fourteenth and subsequent centuries, would be a mere recital of the dissensions of rival chieftains, the feuds of hostile clans, or of the Saxon against the Celt . . ."

So I'd have to move to a larger region. In the year 1506, Connaught, the large mid-coast section of Ireland where we were (including Cong, Galway, Connemara, and the two lakes of Lough Corrib and Lough Mask), was ruled by Hiberno-Norman nobility and powerful Gaelic kings. Though the Vikings and the Anglo-Normans had left their mark, they had been assimilated into the culture and all but disappeared. Connaught itself had never been under the *dominion* of invaders, an historical distinction. In 1506, Ireland was officially under English rule, but in a period of Gaelic resurgence. The area actually under the Crown had shrunk to a small circumference around Dublin known as "the Pale."

Go forward my time away times *one* (1547). Henry VIII has just died. But before he died, he changed his Lordship of Ireland to the more active Kingdom of Ireland. A little earlier, in 1536, Henry VIII broke with English Catholicism in Rome, a terrible portent for Ireland. The change in his designation from "Lord" to "King" of Ireland was the first step in England's effort to make Ireland Protestant. It was a harbinger of Cromwell in the mid-seventeenth century and the suffering and torment that England will inflict upon Ireland for the next four hundred years.

In 1547, Henry's son Edward VI, only ten, inherits the crown and takes his father's wishes further by breaking with papal doctrine altogether. When he dies at sixteen in 1553, his half-sister Mary I, a Roman Catholic holdout, takes the throne, and the state reverts to Catholicism for five years. At Mary I's death, her half-sister Elizabeth I gains the throne, making the definitive break with Rome in 1558. Along the way, the Welsh, the English, and the Scots accept Protestantism for the most part, but not the Irish. In Connaught, the holdouts are many: the native Irish and the group ironically called the "Old English," the descendants of the Anglo-Norman invaders of the 12th century. Staunchly Roman Catholic, they were said to be "more Irish than the Irish themselves."[12] Among their family names are the de Burgs (later Burkes), one of whom owned Annaghkeen Castle in the early fourteenth century.[13]

All of this in four decades, from the start of the sixteenth century to the middle. A drastic shift between two countries— one of ancient tribes and kingdoms with no center, and the other a nascent domineering force—took place in the same amount of time that I'd been away from here. While we had tea at the restaurant, I told Steve; being from an Irish Catholic family, he already knew a fair amount about how the English reformation had affected Ireland, so he wasn't completely amazed at the results of my experiment. As for the other, he knew how long I'd been away from here. I saw in his eyes how much he knew it. Despite how close we are, it was that familiar, quizzical, patient look. There was that hiccup. His view along forty years or five hundred years is a measured, methodical embrace of vast minutiae between rising and setting suns, waxing and waning moons, endless winters that always see a spring and burgeoning summers that inevitably pass into fall. He inhabits time minute to minute, hour to hour, and when the day is done, there will be another or there won't. There are no large gaps, varieties of experience, or extremes. He is unoppressed by it. There's no panic about using it all or making the most of it. Unlike me, he never feels that he must *do* something about it. Maybe because his two parents still live in Southampton, one town over from us. They raised five children and have been married for fifty-seven years. A wider set of parentheses bracket his life, and the second one hasn't even been set down.

In antithetical relation to the information from the pages of books, my overpass memory turned slowly like an ornament, as if in response to the question posed, that of squaring up. Getting it together—getting real. Come *on*, said the span of forty-one years. Get *with it*. Stepping back and looking at four decades was breathtaking, like having been plucked up and shoved along from one stage to the next without ever having realized it, then arriving into the present on a lightning bolt. I would have said *where did it all go*, but that cliché would imply that I wanted to return. There was so much that I wouldn't ever want again. Namely, the frustration of being misunderstood, of being thought inconsequential by almost everyone except my mother, and even her understanding was fraught with problems. The unnamable, untraceable quality of the decades that had passed only served to emphasize how little was different. It *was* implied that we children would be grown-ups one day. Who had told us that? Or was it just that the grown-ups seemed so different, so in control (which they were, but not as much as we thought). Steve sat easy over his teacup, wondering where I had gone to. I shut my eyes, thinking about forty-one years, the forty-one years that were insisting that I conform to them. If anything of real consequence had happened during all that time, well, I'd now be different. I'd now be a grown-up. But I didn't feel changed at all.

"Hey, let's go see Cong," said Steve, with a humorous twinkle in his eye.

Across the road, we found Emmett throwing stones. Above his head, they flew in an arc, one by one, landing in the water with a soft glug. There was still plenty of daylight, a wide sluice of sun on the river's eastern flank. Like a town in the foothills of a mountain range, we could hear water bubbling and coursing almost everywhere. But there were no mountains here. The source is the neighboring lake, Lough Mask, almost as big as Lough Corrib, and thirty-three feet higher. The massive Lough Mask actually vanishes underground at different points along its southern bank and flows for three miles before rising to the surface in pools and streams around Cong. It does this "now you see me, now you don't" act in perpetuity, never failing, so far as history stretches, to drop into the earth and wend its way through subterranean waterways and caves, carving ever larger tunnels and caverns from the limestone. It then surfaces at Cong in the form of this and other rivers before emptying into Lough Corrib.

The mucky bottom was just a few feet down, the water clear as glass. According to the Wilde book, this was once a mill depot to which the Abbey owed its early patronage. The working Abbey had a stone "Fish House" perched about a third of the way out. In the time of the monks, there was a canal beneath it with a fish trap, to which a bell was attached. My mother found this fascinating.

While swimming about in the well the fish would touch a wire which rings a bell in the monastery kitchen. To summon their own executioner, albeit unconsciously, gives a noble cast to the fish's end ...

Looking at the structure, I seriously questioned how the death of a fish could have operatic qualities. This was pure Deborah—morbid, lovable, and sometimes absurd. I hadn't noticed before, but it's impossible to tease the dead. For years, at least in my mind, I wouldn't have dared try. My mother was impervious, unassailable. She was a shrine. Now, I was impatient with her hypersensitivity. I was impatient with her choices, her illusory prison cell. Like a turned-over playing card, it was clear—she didn't even care very much about the fish, or that the monks would be able to eat. She was unable to perceive the simplicity of the moment, apart from the overhang of time.

Now and again, a luckier salmon jumped and landed with a thwack, scattering the sun. Emmett pointed out a beer bottle underwater, bearded in algae. Piles of round stones tufted with mosses and long grasses waved in the current. *The river seems a piece of faultless amber holding the ancient flora of a million years.* This I could understand. It was, it is, and it will be, possibly forever. In the underwater forest, we saw an idling salmon, a wooden crate, and a school of small silver fish in a leaf shape, darting here and there, each in perfect relation to the other.

It was still only about four o'clock, and we had hours of daylight left, a buttery tracing upon slate roof, bright window trim, and chimney pot. The colors almost gave it the feeling of the Mediterranean seaside. I could envision earlier days, women leaning from cottage windows in the afternoon in the springtime air, hanging out their washing. We walked along one curving street that seemed to be the boundary of the entire hamlet. Everything was in miniature, cheerful and fresh, a toy town of the ancients. Next stop, a real café, with fresh-roasted coffee for Steve, a decaf for me, and a hot chocolate for Emmett. We came upon an old-style stone cottage with thatched roof, the type of dwelling that had dotted Ireland coast to coast in the sixties. It was thrilling to see it up close. It was like the Mulloy farm and the other cottages around Annaghkeen that we had often visited in 1965. In fact, this small abode housed the *Quiet Man* museum and is a replica of "White O' Morn," the cottage from the movie that belonged to the Maureen O'Hara character.

We found the tourist shop, an old building of a different style, mortared stone with a slate roof. Over the entranceway, a plaque read "Courthouse, 1853." Time of Trollope, Dickens, Twain. So—153 years old. Only 112 years old when we were here last, 41 years ago. 112 years seemed so mild, so benign, so *contained*. So harmless in relation to these other numbers. Generations really, eons of time were between them: birthdays, dates of death, lumped together Christmases, lifespans of numerous pets, crushes, first days of school, last days of school, first boyfriends, holidays and trips, reunions and heartbreaks whirring by like a film strip in a manic projector or the rifled pages of a book. I thought I'd go back, if only just to have that number again, if only to be that much more removed from the current day. All over again I knew how much I was the same, that my point of view hadn't changed at all. How delightful it would be to walk past this building with its plaque and have it be just 112 years old.

I went in to find an airy little shop with yellow walls and racks of postcards and brochures along them. A woman turned from the cash register behind a long glass counter, a stack of receipt books in her hand. I was hopeful, but not very. Did she know of a castle, a place called Annaghkeen?

"Yes," she said.

"Yes?" I exclaimed.

"Yes," she said, barely noticing my reaction. She ruminated a bit, and eventually she reached under the counter. "I think it's on this map . . ."

She pulled out an ink-and-watercolor reproduction called "CORRIB COUNTRY" and unfolded it. After looking a bit, she pointed with her pencil. "There. There it is. Annaghkeen Castle."

There was the little road, still without a name, coming down to the ragged shoreline of Lough Corrib, ending at the innermost point of an inlet. It said, "Annaghkeen, Eanach Caoin" for the place and then "Annaghkeen Castle (ruin)" closer down to the lakeshore. I asked her to wait a moment and ran to get Emmett and Steve. We gathered around. The thread-like road, drawn in dark purple ink, wound down from Headford in dribs and drabs just as my mother had written.

We passed through a cluster of houses, always taking the left road to reach Annaghkeen . . .

"Emmett, this is where I lived when I was your age!" I exclaimed. At the end of the last turn, in a crook of a small peninsula, a little drawing of a castle looked out over the water in its defensive position, complete with turrets and flags. In the inlet, there was a tiny ink-drawn circle I was sure indicated the island. I put my finger on the spot, "Right here."

While not understanding how long it was since I had been his age (did I any better than he?), or books by people long dead, or books about people long dead, or the Gaelic resurgence and Henry the VIII or forty-one years or five hundred, Emmett knew that finding this ink-drawn castle on the coast of a giant lake was something momentous, that we were near this place in every possible way.

I asked the clerk if Duffy's hardware in Headford was still there, and she said, yes. Paul Duffy, the son, is an estate agent. They would be able to point us in the right direction. She also mentioned that there was a song about Annaghkeen, about a girl. She hummed a tiny bit of it and wished she could remember more. Like the server at the airport, she seemed like some sort of angel. We paid for the map and a few postcards of Ashford Castle, while Steve bought a book on Cong.

I gathered up the purchases, feeling light on my feet. What had been only the name of a book and an idea in my mind was delineated now with a fine purple line on a beautiful map. Annaghkeen was still there. On a map. In the world.

I wondered, what if this were a person? What if this were my mother that I had routed out, managed to steal back from so many years, and we had to try to cover all of the lost time, right here near the Abbey she had thought so beautiful? But people are too complicated. Even my own mother would be too complicated, *especially* her, trying to explain how and why she fell off of time, trying to justify her spectacular cliff dive. It takes too long to understand people, in between what they want you to believe and what they really are, while what they are is always changing. Your job is to read between the lines and try to hang on.

We strolled toward Cong Abbey while Steve thumbed through his book, not alluding to the map discovery. Three weeks on the road, over stream, hill, and dale . . . and we were almost there. He might have thought that the whole thing had been some sort of grand illusion that I had held on to from a childhood fantasy. Yes, there was *Annaghkeen*, though he had never read it. There wasn't much else to prove that it wasn't something I had made out of shreds of a memory, spun up over time into a wedding-cake-sized concoction that kept her with us all along all of these years so she could get more settled and eventually get old.

On either side of the road, Cong Abbey claimed its vault

with skeleton spires as if the road had been jammed right through. Ah, I thought, a ruin is different—different than people. A ruin keeps its pose, pinned against the sky. Firm in its infirmity, its beauty holds.

I used to touch upon the question with a friend who remembered her well. What would my mother have been by now in the mid-aughts? He'd say, oh *come on* . . . She'd have left Peter, found somebody who adored her in an uncomplicated way, given up all of that heavy literature and self-examination, and gotten her furniture at Ikea like everyone else. She'd have become a Zen monk, discovered the internet, and spent hours signing petitions. She'd have a little money and not spend it. But it wouldn't be all Zen and virtue, he said, because she would still be a romantic. Perhaps she'd have resuscitated her French and moved to Europe, married the local vintner in some little town and read late in the afternoon under the wisteria, a glass from the fields at her fingertips. All the while, alive, ordinarily alive, hairs shedding, heart beating, time pulling at her and shaping her like it does everyone.

I didn't point out—and at the time didn't know—that one who has died at the peak of their powers must be aged, must be *made* to be old. It was helpful to think that she'd eventually have blended into the crowd, even more than I could conceive of. I was able to grasp the idea only for moments at a time. Near to impossible, but yes, the protrusions, the extravagances, the jagged spires that a young death leaves would have been worn down and made smooth. She would have become a quirky, upper-middle-class doyenne of the silent generation, mystique fallen away, poking around in the produce aisle, wondering what to have for dinner.

The ruins that she so loved are stuck with a lonely glamour. It drips from their leaning towers, their brown, cragged walls, and their windows to nowhere. No slow, long, and winding decline for them, no lengthy slides toward vacancy. They seem cut off, as if the life went out of them mid-breath, instantly, like the wind is knocked out of a person. There is a sense of fast oblivion, from a living bustling place one day to a cavernous and mournful one the next. By necessity, they've taken time and compressed it, folding it up into ever smaller concentrations. 'Christ, so much of it!' exclaims the ruin. What would you do? Time is perched in a nook, an underground cavern, a musty corner, beckoning to be unfurled.

Through the gothic doorway, we found a blasted birdcage of a structure, open to the sky. Wilde says the doorway was not a part of the original building, but created many centuries later of stones taken from another arch in a fallen wall. There are many fallen walls. He describes the Connaught abbeys as having in fact suffered *less* than the rest of Ireland's religious places from the efforts of England to stamp them out. They were in fact degraded by the attentions of their own people. He paraphrases his predecessor, Caesar Otway, who said that having survived Henry, Elizabeth, and Cromwell, the abbeys unfortunately became victim to their own countrymen—a "busy and fond superstition" that made them highly desired burial sites. He laments the "rooting pigs and rioting boys" that could be found enjoying them unbridled, with no gates to keep them out, no guardians or societies that would look after them. To William Wilde, this was a tragedy.

Inside the door, the nave was paved willy-nilly with tombstones. Of the original structure, only three sides remained, one half crumbled (which we had just traversed), and an opposing wall with one slender window. The best was the high-peaked chancel wall overlooking what was now the road, with three tall thin lights. The array of sepulchers were open to the elements, some ancient, others recent, each marked with a stone of varying degrees of wear. Before Steve could restrain him, Emmett took off, landing first on the stone of Michael Carney, b. 1819, d. 1899, and then to Elizabeth Burke, b. 1826, d. 1894.

With no barriers, the old church was open to interpretation—a gallery of Celtic crosses held straight soldiers, poking up into the sky at angles. They might've been laughing with their heads thrown back. Flat, rectangular tombs had random positions, some still held a shine, some were cracked and dull, at different heights in a bed of gravel. Eruptions of wild green sprang from spaces where the gravel didn't reach. Old, old bones . . . in between the official and unofficial burials that took place here, very likely layers of bones. Graves upon graves upon graves. The most recent arrivals were announced with sharp-cut letters, names, dates, and phrases, and the occasionally decorative filigree—but in general the newer monuments were much more austere than in the days when people spent their lives preparing for eternity.

Steve looked left and right, worried.

"Get down from there!" he yelled.

"There's no one around!" I retorted.

"These places aren't jungle gyms," Steve replied.

"Oh, let a kid have a little fun."

"He should have more respect . . ."

Emmett must have heard the discord and knew his way was clear. His sandaled feet flew around the soldiers, across the granite terrain, from stone to gravel, from slab to slab and back around again.

"You are correct," I said, ". . . and it is also true that we've been a long time on the road . . . And why are we supposed to have reverence for these old things anyway?"

As I often do, I answered my own question.

"Because, in order to feel better about it, we try to be respectful . . . which is really a way of trying to gain control. We feel guilty, so we pay our respects. We bow our heads . . . I'm sorry, we say. We want to contain them; we want to contain ourselves. We expect the next generation to do the same—remember us. My point is that *they* did the same thing for the preceding generation, or maybe they didn't . . . and we will, or maybe we won't, but as you can see, it makes no difference now."

I had not budged him even a little, and I hadn't expected to. As a rule, he doesn't argue about big things, or anything philosophical. For him, it's all wrapped up. He has his own mysterious reality, completely different from mine, and it's incontestable. Perhaps it's because his religious history goes back at least sixteen hundred years, to the time of St. Patrick and the early missionaries, and mine goes back to when my mother started going to Alan Watts lectures on Zen in the sixties.

We stepped through another opening to see a long wall with two windows and three ornamental doors to nowhere. This is thought by some to have been the chapter house of the church. According to Wilde, the row of thin windows across the top signified the second-floor dormitories of the monks, but he didn't venture a guess at what the large downstairs room was. In Wilde's time (before restoration), the wall and doors were covered with brambles and ivy. Now they are clean and open to a green lawn and stone walls that appear to be very slowly melting.

The lack of a ceiling brought my mother to mind, that her favorite idea was to sleep out under the stars. She must have done so as a child because she had a vision of a camp somewhere in the woods on a bright starry night, and it being delicious to look out far away and back in time. The night would be slightly chilly, the scent would be piney, the proximity of roaming beasts only a little frightening. She mentioned it to me often, suggesting it when I went to camp. "Will you get to sleep outside?" she'd prod—as if I, a child on their way to camp, would have any idea what we'd be doing. Eventually, I knew exactly what she was thinking of. It came to me as the dreams of someone close do; it was an imprint, a stamp upon my way of looking at the world. The scene isn't earthy like a Norman Rockwell; it's ethereal, like a Maxfield Parrish. It was a theme of hers, but whether it was she or I who would get to have this treat was not known because in her picture we are interchangeable. Instead of the physical nudity of a Parrish painting, in the picture she is spiritually nude, without preconceptions, or I am. Under the roofless sky and twinkling stars, in the endless night, we can each substitute for the other. But we aren't there together. I am alone there, and she is somewhere else. Or she is there, and I am here.

Current science tells us that stars are ghosts of their former incarnations. Having died out long ago, we can still see them burn. Time is a fourth dimension, relative to matter and more elastic. Time is like a fabric, we are told, along with space. Massive objects like the pyramids drag on it. It has tiny flaws called wormholes that theoretically can connect different points within it. It is pliable, relative to perception, and perception is relative to where we are. In our experience, we can't be two places in space-time at once, but the behavior of much smaller entities demonstrates just that possibility. Laws of nature are assumed to be "time symmetrical," meaning that time should be able to go forward *or* backward, but causal estimations of time show that though we may have an influence on the future, we can't change the past. A child is conceived and then born, not the other way around. Milk and coffee mixed together easily produce a beige liquid, but we can't un-mix them without a complicated process in a chemistry lab. Time seems to go *forward*, which makes it asymmetrical, though there are some "philosophers of the manifold" who think that is merely a function of our own peculiar perceptions.

It's called "Time's Forward Arrow."[14] We know it, we live it every day. Indeed, to the unexperienced, the asymmetry seems suspect, unbalanced. Weird. That is why children hound us with questions about it, their concept of themselves and their world newly fragmented by beginnings and endings, those irrefutable marking points. They must learn it; they must acclimate to it like we did. They seem obtuse while we tell them again and again, forgetting that at one time the knowledge wasn't commonplace to us either. A dim distant light that haunts us: our own earliest years, the inexpressible state before we saw ourselves and our surroundings as finite on either end and time wasn't such an enemy.

According to these philosophers of the manifold, time works the same either way, forward or backward. The asymmetry that we perceive is only a *learned* observation, and in fact every future event is set in stone, like the past. Time is symmetrical, they say, true to laws of physics. If this is true, and in fact we don't determine anything, at least as the future happens we have the *illusion* of choice, a sharp contrast to the seemingly intractable nature of what is "behind us." Maybe that's why we hang around places like Cong Abbey—the balance is off. Under the impression that we can at all times be self-determining, we want to correct it. We want it to work both ways. We're looking for some sort of clue.

Through the freestanding wall, a wide lawn gently dropped toward the river. Brief fragments of the cloister bracketed the green double columns that formed gothic arches in a pilaster style. Their capitals were ringed with carvings described in

Wilde's book as floral, but to me they're more like whorls of cake frosting: each one different, figures piped in ganache or fondant, the sharp edges and symmetry a surprise in the tableau of worn stone. With a little imagination, we were able to picture the arcade whole, design variations multiplied or repeated along the arches, enclosing the square. Outside of the fragments ran a gravel path to show where the monks once walked a thousand years ago.

We circled around, keeping our eyes on Emmett, occasionally glimpsing him through one of the window holes behind us. Steve called him down. I was sure that Emmett would be interested to hear about Roderic O'Connor, the last High King of Ireland, who called this place home a mere jot before us, only 850 years ago. I then questioned what that could mean to him. Emmett jumped onto a near monument, then shuffled his feet before disembarking, flying through the air. He never thinks, "What does it matter, Mom? I've got so much," or "I've got so little." He's only *right now*. That is because time is his friend. He isn't separate from it. He hasn't bunched it up into future piles, been desirous of anything beyond his birthday or an ice cream cone, or had more than the most fleeting thought about what happened "before." Emmett especially is not covetous, forgetting about presents I had hoarded away from an overabundant Christmas, and leaving his things, books, change, rocks, shells, candy, anything that was beloved for a moment all over the house and the classroom. There is no future moment that he's cordoned off, no past that he wishes he could reverse, beyond a dog named Boo that died, and even that hasn't taken up a permanent position in his head. When he sees a picture of Boo, it's as if he's stepped into another room. And then he steps back again, returns into the flow of time, not fighting it, not trying to change it or catch up with it.

Yet for us, time contracts and expands, making us seasick. We wander through its crumbling walls, desolation, and piles of knocked-down stones. We are looking for the bit that tells—memories of a starry sleep that never happened, or in icing scrolls on stone fragments. A light seems to emanate from them. How could this be? So long ago. All the more eloquent for the creep of vine, the lichen flower collage, the sandy, fossil-pocked granite and limestone. We want to know—how old is this place really? Cong Abbey was founded by St. Fechin in the early seventh century says The Irish Association Survey. Quill pens just introduced; English barely invented. But William Wilde claims the spindly skeleton behind us was founded by the Augustinians in approximately 1128, after a fire burned down the older building. To him, it was 739 years old. To us, if we use his dates, it is 878 years old. If we use the Irish Survey, it was 1325 years old, but it *is* 1380 years old. Which is true? It turns out to be relative. The only thing about which there is no question—we are all of us along a continuum that seems to go in one direction only.

Emmett caught up with us, the glitter of adventure playing about his face. We had left the cloister and were in the avenue of yews, on our way down to the riverside. Facts and figures will never be certain. But still I had a sense of that contemplative person, perhaps my mother, walking along under the arcade, looking up now and then, or taking a stool into the center of the atrium to read, thinking of the same sorts of things that we were. I wondered what she would think of our trek, that we had been over six hundred miles and through ten counties, and that, if all went according to plan, I'd soon be back at the island. Out of all the people I knew, those with me and those departed, she would have understood it the best. That we were here would have pleased her greatly because when we left Ireland, she wanted there to be a future for me here, at least of some kind.

I pictured her walk, stopping to jot down her thoughts in one of the composition books that were the start of *Annaghkeen*, seeing the silvered sable color of the river through the trees. The tone of *Annaghkeen* tells what she felt, that whatever innocence any of us had was going to be short-lived. And now, having had so much rise to the surface, I knew it too. Yet as we approached the river, chattering its gentle descent from Lough Mask to Corrib, I felt that all was not lost—that *we* were not. Just by being here and thinking about her, or any person along the time continuum, we've shone a light into the darkening past. Who is to say that they do not sense us there?

The Storybook

The clear sunlight falls on the hill and fresh white clouds blow about the sky. Mr. Mulloy is cultivating in the fields on the hill. I can see his back over the green rows of sugar beets. Above the wall the green barley waves in the wind and the haystacks are omphali in the sun.

Two boys from California with fantastic hair styles stay up with Luke for the horse racing in the lounge. Their French father, having left Carmel earlier for a visit to France, will meet the family in Cobh... This is another fact that will shape a different breed: the world is casual to these children, while to us it was a storybook. When we grew up and got to the places in the book, we imposed the story as long as possible.

I remember narrow roads of dirt and stone around Annaghkeen. Often, we had to stop to wait for farmers, cows, sheep, and pigs in extended families. Yesterday, it happened again while we were looking for the castle. For about a quarter mile, we were slowed to a crawl by a herd of sheep. Packed together tightly, their options were few. We puttered behind them until they found a way over the rise into an open pasture, their high wooly butts bouncing like bowls of cottage cheese. The sight was so familiar I thought we must be in the right place. I was taken in by the atmosphere, by the feel of something as opposed to the facts, and not for the first time in my life.

Though the area looked familiar, when we got down to the shore, there was no castle. We tried a few different roads, attempting to orient ourselves with the map. It was hard to tell because most ended at the lake and had no signage. Lough Corrib is twenty-seven miles long and ten miles wide; we were dots on its shore. So we went up to Headford to see if we could find Duffy's hardware store.

Duffy's had a sign with old-fashioned letters and the latest in lawn mowers and water toys out on the sidewalk. Inside, a tall teenager was looking at some tool books. A quick scan showed the place to have survived because it was thoughtfully laid out—walls of pegboards with farm machine parts and all manner and sundry of tools for the building boom. The Duffy family was also selling properties; a sign for "Duffy's Auctioneers and Estates" was posted.

While we were poking around, three men from the village came in for *craic* (pronounced "crack"), which is what they call conversation here. In *Annaghkeen*, my mother chastises herself for getting caught in social situations and talking too much to fill up space. I do it too, usually to fill up what I perceive as emptiness or no context. I'm driven to make a context if there is none, and sometimes the only way to do it is to divulge too much, to push past the demarcation line. Maybe I just want to make an impression. Which I then regret because I've talked too much.

I listened to the rhythm. How do they do it? To begin with, craic is light but can be tinged with regret. The feelings of people making the craic are muted and on a distant shore. This isn't cynicism; it is the reason craic can go on and on, without any effort or, apparently, any misgivings. Among the older generation, the tacit agreement is that everything will stay on a small scale. The second rule is that they never talk about themselves very much, and the third is that they never talk about anything earnestly. Craic is a smooth flow of words that goes straight from brain to tongue; the speaker navigating through other streams of craic like a car weaves in and out of traffic on an expressway. There are rarely any accidents or spills because everyone stays in their lane. Their accents were so thick I couldn't tell what they were talking about.

A man with fine smooth skin and wispy hair was behind a window at the back of the store. When he came out, I asked for Kevin Duffy, whom I guessed was his father. He introduced himself as Paul Duffy and said that Kevin was on vacation in Austria with his mother. Kevin had just gotten back, in fact. *But we must not think too much about these matters . . .* Kevin Duffy, whom I had emailed in the winter about the island, thinking I was emailing his wife Josephine, and again divulging too much.

Paul Duffy was busy but seemed determined to be polite. I got out my map from the tourist's office and my copy of *Annaghkeen* and told him the story. I showed him the picture of Deborah in the back of the book and mentioned T. C. J. and Nancy O'Connell, the owners of the island. Oh yes, he knew the place, and it seemed as though he knew the book too. The O'Connells had passed on, and their son Bob owned the island now, he said. I added that I had heard that news from Kevin by email. We had looked into the possibility of renting the house on the island through Kevin, but the O'Connells weren't interested.

Awash in a sea of my own emotion, I still was able to see Paul's complete inability to sort through the intimate threads of my life. The Irish have to work at catching up with the goal -orientation of an American. Two things get in their way: the first is a natural resistance to intimacy, the second is pace. They can't get there as fast as you can. They might never get there. The older ones don't attempt to broach the gap, but instead smile indulgently at your foolishness and mention something about the weather. No doubt the fine fellows in the front of the store would have done the same had I spilled out my tale for them.

"Is the island still there? The house?" I rushed along, talking too fast because of the excitement of being so close to an actual live person from those days that wasn't my father or Luke. Paul was like a man trying to paw out of a big cobweb while being graceful about it. He seemed amazed at this story galloping at him from 1965, the year of his birth. He emphasized that fact more than once, as if to absolve himself of responsibility, while I was definitely not staying in my conversational lane. Yes, he said, the island was still there, and so was the house. I could hardly believe it. We were so close now.

Steve and Emmett came in from their meander down the main street. Paul took my name down, and the names of Deborah and Peter, writing them slowly in a book so he could give them to his parents. He was probably relieved to see I had a husband and a child. He said he wanted a copy of *Annaghkeen* (did he?). I said I would send him one while he took a real-estate flyer from the displays for the address. One of the flyers advertised the Ower House Hotel.

"Yes!" I exclaimed. "The Ower House Hotel! This is where they heard the singing—the Irish National Anthem and 'Danny Boy.' There are pages on it. Then they sang it in the car all the time, crying. That is—'Danny Boy' . . . not the Irish National Anthem."

Now I had jumped my lane and crashed into the median. Paul searched for something tangible on which to hang a sentence. I could have it, he said, meaning the Ower House Hotel, for 1,000,000 euro.

"Oh yeah, sure," I joked. "We'll take it."

I asked him if his parents might want a visit and understood from him that they might in a few days, after they had rested up.

"Is the island very hard to find?"

"No, it isn't. Very easy."

"Maybe we'll go have a look and come back to see if your dad is here? I'd love to say hello, even if it's from a long time ago."

"Ahh yes, sure. He might be in. Stop by . . ."

"Yes . . . I uh . . . well, I've gotten an idea to write a book, a companion book to *Annaghkeen*. First, I have to go to all the places."

"You'll have no problem finding it," he said and drew us a little map.

In the car, Steve channeled Paul Duffy. "So be off with ye!" Which I didn't think was entirely true, though I didn't know for sure.

After a few minutes, we came to a little group of cottages that the road ran straight in between. Upon seeing them, I knew for the first time we were not far from the castle. I remembered them absolutely. They were so close to the road that while passing we could have reached out and plucked a bloom from a windowsill.

One cottage was next to a barn, across the road from another row of ramshackle barns and another cottage. They were of plaster daub, the roofs corrugated tin; the front doors were no more than two feet from the road. With no sidewalk, it was like an old Italian town where a pedestrian zone has been created. But here there was traffic—like us. Taken with the moment, I pulled over next to a stone wall laced with orange rowan berries and pink roses. We popped Emmett onto the wall and took a picture.

One house, lime-washed in daub with a roof of thatch, was next to one of bare cement, but all had attached stables, sheds, and a barn-yard walled around them. Philomena later said the name of the place was Knocklaher.

I slipped past the rickety barns and broached the façade of the first house. I looked in the window and saw an old woman. The door was ajar, so I knocked gently and pushed it open. She was tending to something on the stove in a thin housedress, her hunched back to us. She turned to me with dull eyes.

"Is Annaghkeen this way?" I asked, pointing against the traffic.

She nodded wordlessly in answer to a question that had been asked of her a thousand times. She knew that "they" knew where the lake was, or where Annaghkeen Castle was, but stopped to ask because they were sightseeing, and this an-cient enclave smack on the road pulled them in the same way it pulled me in.

And I hadn't been the only one.

The doors of Irish cottages always stand open on summer days, unless the people are away; I went into the nearest. A toothless an-cient turned from the stove, and confirmed our route.

As interlopers in 1965, we were a curious and inconvenient note in the lives of the people who had been here for centuries. To think—forty-one years later I stopped there because I remembered it and because it looked Irish in an old-fashioned way. As with Muckross, we hadn't planned it and only found the coincidence while reading through *Annaghkeen* a few mornings later. The woman I spoke to was probably the grown-up child of the original toothless ancient, and now a toothless ancient herself. The only change from then to now was that the thatch roof had been replaced by a tin one.

We drove on, referring to Paul Duffy's map and also my mother's directions. Incredibly green fields stretched from stone wall to stone wall. Even at moments where it seemed counterintuitive, we bore left, *always taking the left road . . .* as per *Annaghkeen* and the map. Small herds of cows were grazing, while honey-colored light angled over the fields, turning silvery in the tall grasses along the stone walls. The smell was warm and steady through the car windows: cow pie and sun.

And there it was. Steve pointed it out first, a square stone structure the shape of a latch plate in a vast green field, with another ruin just to the east of it, almost as big. We glided toward them, strips of metallic blue appearing behind the field and on either side. It was perfect that Steve saw them first. Without him, I never would have been able to return.

The road crunched under the tires, the castle disappearing and reappearing as we came around the bend, as did the lake, silver-blue, then bronze, then blue again. The castle to our left, now a few hundred feet away, was small and majestic. The house, about sixty yards offshore on the island, was tranquil as a museum. It all looked pretty much the same.

I stared up at the castle and surveyed the whole. The island trees were bigger, the landscaping more elaborate than before.

Though it was summer, there were no people. No forgotten toys on the grass. No dog-eared books on the picnic table. No boat waiting oars-akimbo from a quick trip to the store. No cars parked near ours.

The whole place seemed captured by the sun and held still, while light like broken glass sprang from the surface of the lake. The castle was rough and gray, sun-pounded, austere. Humble and crude, walls six feet thick. A few cows grazing looked over at us with soft eyes. I looked all the way to the top. The closer I got, the bigger it was. A blazing sphere winked from the edge of stone.

We arrived back on the lawn and took a drink in the bright sunshine. The children were swimming and diving off the wall into the clear bronze water.

The house looked barely changed from the book-jacket picture. Did it look smaller, as things are supposed to when you haven't seen them since childhood? No. Scraggly-armed pines had filled in, and there were many more plantings. As well as *Annaghkeen*, I had one of my mother's color pictures of the house. The windows had been changed; they were slightly bigger. The sun porch was rebuilt in a different style, though close to the same size. No second story, no new wings. A loved place that resided in someone's imagination, a person who lived in Dublin whom I've never met, who didn't want to rent to me, descended from another person, deceased, whom I can barely remember except as a perhaps not altogether flattering sketch in *Annaghkeen*. These were the people that had real lives here.

Steve peered at me watchfully.

The atmosphere was tightly woven, packed with information. It seemed to me that my mother had put a frame around the castle and the island. The retaining wall that Lukie and I had dived from was grown over with bushes and ivy. To the right, the dock and the landing where I'd had my rowing lessons from him before the Braider kids arrived and usurped our routine. I thought of Jackson Braider, when we spoke of our parents and that summer. He was another who said, "Old times, Rue . . . old times . . ." snapping me back into the present.

Emmett was in the field in between the two ruins, dwarfed by monuments of stone, and now a book-jacket castle looked out over a cloud-torn sky, the colors black and white and all gradations in between—the style so impressionistic the forms were lost at close range. I left Steve and Emmett and walked out down the little road to the bend where it carried around the curve of the lake. We would have had this perspective coming in from a day on the boat. Warring, very likely. Usually fallen out into two halves: Dad and Luke in their corner of the outboard, Mom and me in ours. Sometimes Luke and Dad having an argument, or just Mom and Dad. Everyone relieved when the boat got to the dock, scraping up odds and ends and stuffing them in the picnic basket—spent bottles, binoculars, gathered rock fossils, bird guides. Except for me. I didn't want to get away from anyone. I had no idea that in between thrown-together meals, swimming, and watching old movies on TV Éireann, my mother was making her picture: hammering together the frame, stretching a thick canvas.

The grass gleamed by the roadside, each blade a shining individual in the sun. The light of Ireland reveals the separateness of the petal from the flower, and the texture of the bog, and the eyes of the cow . . . Is it the tiny prisms of rainwashed air that light up the land? One sees too well. It is heartbreaking.

Each thing is distinct from the other, each blade of grass and flower has done its work and is now finished. To create the picture was to pull all the pieces together in the frame, hold them still upon the canvas. It was to defeat the distance between herself and my father, herself and her own body, herself and the God that she had hoped for, herself and her children who changed constantly, becoming their own individual selves. In the face of it, she pulled tight the cloth, selected her pencil, and began to sketch out our time.

My father was different. Ireland was a pit stop, a strange flavor, a blip upon the surface of the years when his career was really materializing. Ireland was the two of them in the red VW, singing "Danny Boy," my mother crying, even my father crying, which didn't often happen—one tear finding a way down his craggy cheek. My brother Luke, sitting in the back with arms crossed, incredulous at the whole scene.

My father wasn't very involved with us, though he liked that we were there. He wrote all the time. He was never very connected with any of his family during the whole of his life, except for Alex. But in Ireland, he hadn't made the later arrangements. He hadn't yet formed the old turtle's hide. He hadn't yet said, "You take this, and I'll take that, and that's the deal." His later life and art were areas hermetically sealed from each other, yet here was an estuary in between, a place of occasional flooding. He was still giving it a try, putting his heart into it. The flooding didn't happen often, yet when it did, his vivid presence, his tenderness and intensity of feeling were exceptional. He was extremely hard to reach, except on the subject of language. He lived for language, for the magic of it.

A lifetime of translating universal experience into art had placed his own relations with others on a sort of permanent remove. The master wordsmith was largely hidden behind words.

Now and again, he'd see with crystal clarity what he had done or not done, what he had missed, and how that person had been affected. It would hit him like a thunderbolt. One time, feeling bad about the way he had treated me, he spent some extra time with me on the island, time for me and me alone. We sat on the bed, and he queried me at length about my troll collection. That was genuine, his saving grace. He also did it in Italy, on LSD. He was kind out of remorse, but the affection was real. Later, when I didn't live with him anymore, my life got much easier.

About "Danny Boy," he said, "Imagine telling someone, 'Tis *I'll* be here in sunshine or in shadow . . .'" He loved the remove of the line. The singer's acknowledgement of the permanence of sad circumstances. The humbleness of it, the resignation—into love, into fate, into life. The trap of intensely felt longing and romantic love that would not be fulfilled. Not open-ended, not joyful, but most keenly felt in partings and endings. Perfect for a person who was not there most of the time, even when they were in the same house or sitting across from you at dinner.

Apart from many other wonderful and worthwhile qualities, my father was like a contagion that found a willing host in my mother. From the beginning, he was willing to take a risk on her because she interested him, though he hadn't yet had the experience of living with someone of equal ambition. As his epic complexity became apparent to her, so did his inadvertent cruelty, and the loneliness of living with someone more committed to an aesthetic than the people around him.

The person my father was touched her deeply; she understood the particular way that he was saving himself. Like her, he was mercurial, but for different reasons. He was enormously self-determined, so he was always pulling away, toward his perfection in art. In the beginning, he was in love with her, which slowly morphed into an idea of a purity that could not survive in the earthly realm, which then translated into literature, and then transferred back to her when she was dying. She was drawn to the power of poetry and precise articulation, but an aesthetic wasn't enough for her. She hadn't made the compromise that he had—to fit around it, to make it the center of things. She was going for more, which made her impossible to deal with, but which was revolutionary in its way.

Within the parameters he had set for himself, he was alone, and he made the people around him feel alone too. We all sacrificed. To my mother, these frustrations were prosaic, almost foretold. The further he got out there on his self-created planet, the more intimately involved she became, not so much in a bid for his attentiveness as in an inquiry into the nature of what had gone wrong. It's there in her words that make the picture, that go in the frame . . .

. . . *each blade a shining individual in the sun . . . One sees too well . . .*

From her distant perch, she has reverence for him and for the separateness of us all. She cannot merge, she cannot join in, in the way she most desires to. It is heartbreaking. The world is slowly turning from her, carrying on without her.

As I walked back to the castle, a few boys with fishing poles went by me on bikes. I turned to see Steve climbing the stone steps up the bank.

Here was just yesterday. The field where I was chased by a bull. The dock where Lukie gave me rowing lessons. The leprechaun dens, the pine-bark fires, Cloaca Maxima and Cloaca Minor. The tiny blankets I knitted with Philomena.

At close range, the picture was obscured again. Inside the

castle door, watery ribbons of sun came through cracks in the stone. Through an impressionistic veil, I was able to see the original pure idea. That was what the wager had been about—going for an *idea* that they had, that everyone had. In this, Deborah and Peter were united. All the way and without reservations. I could feel it in my bones. In its unpolluted, early state, it was a fairy tale without the villain. It was a world unshackled from constraints and held to a standard of fairness (by whom, I would later wonder). It was where, once the restraints were removed, human nature would naturally default to a kind of utopia. For the American history books, it could be loosely categorized as a cycle of naivete, hope, and upheaval that was most purely expressed at the beginning of the sixties revolution. What child wouldn't love it? A storybook world without guilt, or wars, or violence. No valuations, no compromises . . . *a buoyant bath of pure melting and unimaginable distinctions . . .* That's what we were all going for together. My father took away Zen, which provided the balance that he so desperately needed. Through Zen, my mother attempted salvation, and perhaps she found it.

I picked through knee-high grass to the center of the ruin, looking all the way to the top, stone by stone, trying to imagine how many floors it had and where the lookout was. This stacked puzzle of granite had stood for centuries without mortar, just because of the way it fit together. Close and pixelated now, like looking through oil-splattered glass. I turned and turned; Emmett running by was a filament across the bottom of a window. The coolness of shadowed stone encircled me. The original idea stayed with me a minute more before it flew off under the cynical gaze of the present.

Our attention was arrested by a small white sedan that came thundering around the corner of the Annaghkeen road, a cigarette resting in the nicotine-stained fingers on the steering wheel. A convivial face and eyes twinkled with either malice or welcome, we couldn't tell which. For the intents and purposes of the driver, the lakeside road that went up to the last house ended when his foot hit the brake. Steve came down the steps. The driver hadn't budged; he seemed to be waiting for us to speak.

We introduced ourselves, and I offered up the book as the reason for being here in case he was the owner of something. He gave *Annaghkeen* a quick look and identified himself as Mattie Kenney. As he got out of his car, he handed the book right back to me. He seemed to have only a passing interest in our details. He threw out his cigarette and offered me one, which I accepted while he lighted another for himself. He stood close to light mine. I instantly felt like he was an old friend. This was another instance of the easy familiarity that some of the men here have with women they have never met. I dragged on the cigarette which made my head spin. I rolled down the roster of names from *Annaghkeen*: Duffys (yes), Philomena Fahey (so many Faheys, so many Philomenas), Father Keane (died a long time ago), King's Store (gone a long time), Joyce's who delivered groceries to us (they have a big market and gas in town now).

"Joyce's! Where we turned toward the lake!" I exclaimed.

"Do you take a drink?" he asked me and Steve.

"Well, I do," I said, looking to Steve.

Steve shook his head and said, "Gave that up a long time ago."

Mattie Kenney nodded as if that were a smart thing to do, though he hadn't taken his own advice. "My wife left me not too long ago," he said to us apologetically. "It was the gambling too. Are you goin' to the races?"

He meant the Galway races, which were in full swing. I said

that we wanted to but needed a guide. Maybe we could pick him up and we could go together? But I had jumped my conversational lane again.

He said he might meet us there. "Go on Thursday. Today is the hat day. Thursday's the day to go."

I was sorry that we couldn't take him up on the drink, but it was clear that he was taking Steve's lead. He might have felt awkward to be drinking with me while my husband drank soda. Steve wouldn't have minded. In *Annaghkeen*, everyone is always going over to other people's houses for drinks and having chats about books. And England, lots about England, which no longer seemed to be a central concern.

Now, living like that seemed quaint, as well as highly dysfunctional. It also seemed alcoholic. I miss those times. Is it wrong to miss alcoholism? Oh, I know how serious it is. It killed my biological father. It was a great encumbrance for Steve before he straightened himself out. But I miss the whole devil-may-care aspect of it. I miss the lordly squandering of life's riches. The sexy part, before things get disgusting. The Tennessee Williams part, early in the play. The abandon, the refusal to be very careful. The loosened clothes, the honest words, the flushed faces, and thundering laughter. The warmth, the high. The immortal feeling. The bravado. The secrecy, the lusts. The keen knife edge of narcissism, where the boundaries of self are cartoon sharp. Not blank. Not vague. Not wishy-washy. Not quiet, not Zen. I miss the part that doesn't last. But what does last? Nothing.

How do I know this?

It's hard to watch one's mother floating around in an olive grove looking at her hand or tearing up boxes that have faces drawn on them that are supposed to be *her* mother, or one's father going for a swim on LSD and needing to be rescued because he thought he was a fish, and believe in any such thing as permanence.

Leafing through my notes, I pointed to the small farmhouse on the hill and said, "The Mulloy farm, is that it?"

"'Tis," he said, looking pleased.

"That's where we got our milk and eggs," I said as his face came to life.

Mattie Kenney seemed to know everything there was to know about the Mulloys. There were five Mulloy sisters, and Pat, the only son. Three of the sisters had gone to the St. Louis area, he said. I mentioned that my mother was from St. Louis, a fact that had no relevance to him.

I asked if the farm was still whole, and Mattie said no. With six kids inheriting, many pieces had been sold off and probably only seven or so acres were still farmed. Some had become lots along the Annaghkeen road, which were for sale. He pointed to a field to the left of the house, overlooking Lough Corrib. This piece was owned by Pat, his childhood best friend, who was almost exactly his age. I volunteered that Pat Mulloy got quite a lot of coverage in *Annaghkeen*, though this fact wasn't of interest to Mattie either. "Each of the kids got a piece," he added, looking a bit wistful.

In a conversation about the Mulloys, my mother wrote, Father Johnson, a local priest, disapproved of what he termed Pat's "lack of ambition." She responded to this in the journal that would become *Annaghkeen*:

I thought of Pat's handsome, virile face, of Pat fishing for trout and perch in the lake, of Pat climbing the mountain with his friends, of his inheriting, as the only son, the whole of his old father's thirty acres, and could find nothing to lament.

So the patriarchal model had been done away with after all, one of the few of her predictions that didn't come true.

Mattie gestured again to the piece of waterfront overlooking the island house. "Pat had called it for himself, an acre, and always intended to build there," he said and paused, while we did too, waiting for what came next.

"Last year, he died in his house in Baltimore," he said.

Steve and I gasped.

He was "gassed," Mattie added, which we didn't understand, so I asked him to elaborate.

"You know how when they put the car in the house?" he asked incredulously. "He left the car on and went to do a few things . . ."

I realized that this notion would seem intrinsically odd to most older Irish, who probably equate a car with horses and would no more put a car in the house than they would move their families into the barn.

He seemed sad about this for a moment and then he asked, "Are those your real teeth?"

"Yes," I said. He shook his head with wonder at American dentistry.

We talked about Annaghkeen Island itself, that the O'Connells' son who owns it is "a surgeon in Dublin too."

As for the Mulloys, they remained "all around here . . ." he said, gesturing wide. Mattie's sons had built on some of the Mulloy lots, and those houses weren't selling. He seemed somewhat exasperated and bewildered at this. His son Eugene was buying lots at 300,000 euro for each, which he could hardly believe.

He offered me another cigarette, and I accepted in order to keep the conversation going. This was more than my usual one-a-day. I felt woozy. I wished that we could have a civilized setting to talk, instead of standing in the driveway. The whole interchange was beginning to have a rushed and frantic feeling, like most of my conversations in the States. Ideas and tidbits went back and forth at an ever more accelerated rate until we came to the inevitable subject of markets. Which made me wonder, were markets now driving *all* of our conversations? As well as the entire globe? Was the subject inevitable because it was the *last subject* in a long line of them, the miserable apex toward which all indicators pointed?

"The Celtic Tiger hit four or five years ago, and the whole thing went cracked," Mattie said, eyes wide. He pointed to the island. "Worth at least 1.5 million now. O'Connells bought it for 950 pounds. *950 pounds.*"

We shook our heads with wonder at these phenomenal gains. I told him it was much the same story in the States; no one had ever seen the like.

I said that I had tried to rent the house and island from Dr. O'Connell. Mattie seized upon this moment to say I could rent his house if I wanted to. Anytime. He described it, and I knew it as one of the new houses up on the Annaghkeen road. I remembered that it had a thatch roof.

"Built just last year," he said. Out of the four or five bungalow-style houses, it was the only attractive one.

Mattie stayed a little while more and then thundered off. We stood in a cloud of dirt and dust spitting off his wheels.

"Well, I guess Paul Duffy sent him down here," Steve said.

"Heading us off at the pass," I said, feeling a little bit dazed still from the smoking.

Steve looked at me. "How are you?" he asked.

"I don't know how I am."

Suddenly, we were at the end of August, at the end of our trip, which was strange and shocking.

Nobody watches me like Steve. When I am far away, nobody would know except for him. He doesn't know where I go and fundamentally isn't that interested. But he knows the basics: It's 1965, I am seven years old. I am forty-eight, it's 1965. I am forty-eight, it is today. I am seven, it is today.

The Mulloy farmhouse was still standing, white and contained up on the rise around the bend. Once, I got close to a tinker father and daughter at the Mulloys'. The tinkers had taken over a nearby field, their painted wagons in a semi-circle at the back of the clearing. We'd drive by, seeing the adults tending to the cooking fires, the children playing, a few shaggy ponies grazing, maybe one or two kids riding the ponies or grooming them. So near to us, the effect was striking. They were lifted from legend; as if a curtain had risen on an ancient play. From our VW, I plagued my parents: What are these kids like? Do they go to school? Who owns the ponies? Is it summer all year long? Does everyone have a pony? Can we visit? No matter how much I begged, we were not going to go and say hello. But the tinkers were living *outside*, which was to me as good an invitation to "come over" as there could possibly be. We're NOT going to stop, they said.

Later, my mother and I were at the Mulloy farm, getting our milk and eggs. I will never forget the square plaster walls of their kitchen. The front door opened right into it. There was a decoration on the wall that fascinated and horrified me. A hanging cross with Jesus nailed on it. He was a thin, sylph-like Jesus, with strange ochre skin tones. His head hung to one side with great sorrowful eyes. His hands and feet were nailed to the cross, dripping with red blood. I had never seen anything like it.

Mrs. Mulloy had given me a glass of milk warm from the cow. There was a knock at the door, and she got up to answer.

I peered past her and saw two tinkers from the camp. I recognized them immediately, a man and a girl about thirteen. They had that smudged, wild look, their eyes held away. They didn't want anything from Mrs. Mulloy except to sell her some things. They could have been stand-ins for what my father and I later became after Mom was gone. They, too, were compatriots by necessity, bewildered visitors to a "real" Real Life where they uncomfortably found themselves. A father and daughter forced together, affectionate but at odds. Out on the road stood their horse-drawn wagon, waiting to take them back to the distant, fabled place of my imaginings.

In August of 1965, something was ending—more than any of us could have realized. In the beginning of *Annaghkeen*, my mother listed their recent accomplishments. As always, the simple facts are shadowed by their finite nature, their edges blurring into the larger picture she was painting.

We have finished some things, a beautiful book has been written, a beautiful baby born, a splendid house built; but it is not those that have ended, but some as yet unarticulated phase of my life, and theirs willy-nilly. Or his life and mine willy-nilly.

And here again something was ending. Steve touched my arm. I looked at the house, picturing the inside from memory. A curtain on the window. A ladder to the attic. The glassed-in porch. The old TV. Mildewed books. My brother Luke and I fighting over who got to drink the salad dressing left in the bottom of the bowl. The monkey puzzle tree. My troll collection. My mother, almost always in a skirt. A long leg to hug. My sharp-faced, unpredictable father, surprisingly warm at times, callous at others. All determined by mysterious rhythms into which we were inhaled and expelled like dandelion seeds. Yet there were ways to hold together—if only by proximity to each other, by crawling back into the arms of the other, by being accepted.

. . . the world is casual to these children, while to us it was a story-book. When we grew up and got to the places in the book, we imposed the story as long as possible.

For all her ruminations, she didn't know that the world wasn't casual to us. As much as they were in earnest, we were too. As serious, if undefined. As feeling, if not sentimental. When we left Annaghkeen, the storybook ended. The childhood she longed to re-create . . . *a buoyant bath of pure melting and unimaginable distinctions* . . . was left behind. Here.

Acknowledgments

I am grateful to Peter Ginna and Maria Matthiessen for their comments on the early drafts of this book, and their enthusiasm for it. Each of their emails produced a eureka moment for me—something in the bubbling cauldron I had created had tasted good. The wonderful folks at *Kestrel* published an excerpt, another shot of invaluable and much-needed support. Patricia Hampl, and later Lance Richardson, said I must not give up. My brothers Lucas Matthiessen and Alex Matthiessen read and cheered me on, as did many friends too numerous to mention. Editors Jane Rosenman and Henry Gifford gave me great notes and meticulous editing. I especially want to thank Jon Gosch and Latah Books for taking me on.

And for my husband Steve Shaughnessy, who understood that I have to write, I am filled with gratitude. He is a source of great strength.

Lastly, I want to thank my father, who sits on my shoulder when I write, and always said I could do it.

Notes

1. Cavalleri, "Scientific Reports," Royal College of Surgeons (RCSI), University of Edinburgh, 2017

2. McCann, May, Séamas Ó Síocháin and Joseph Ruane, eds. *Irish Travellers: Culture and Ethnicity*. Belfast: Institute of Irish Studies, 1994

3. McCann, May, Séamas Ó Síocháin and Joseph Ruane, eds. *Irish Travellers: Culture and Ethnicity*. Belfast: Institute of Irish Studies, 1994

4. Report of the Commission on Itinerancy. Government Publications Office. August, 1963

5. Macalister, Robert. *Ireland in Pre-Celtic Times*. Dublin: Maunsel and Roberts, 1921

6. O'Brien, Maire and Conor Cruise. *A Concise History of Ireland*. London: Thames and Hudson, 1980

7. McCaffrey, Carmel. *In Search of Ancient Ireland*. Chicago: New Amsterdam Books, 2001

8. Yeats, William Butler. *Irish Folk Stories and Fairy Tales*. London: Walter Scott Publishing Co., 1888

9. Selver, Charlotte. "Report on Work in Sensory Awareness and Total Functioning." 1968

10. Wilde, William Robert. *Lough Corrib*. Dublin: McGlashan & Gill, 1867

11. "Roderic O'Connor." *Encyclopedia Britannica.* January 1, 2021

12. "'More Irish than the Irish themselves' (Hiberniores Hibernisipsis)." In *The Oxford Companion to Irish History* (2nd ed.), ed. S.J. Connolly. Oxford: Oxford University Press, 2002

13. Wilde, William Robert. *Lough Corrib.* Dublin: McGlashan & Gill, 1867

14. "Time." *Encyclopedia Britannica.* 1999

Bibliography

How the Irish Saved Civilization. Cahill, Thomas. 1995

Irish Folk Tales. Curtin, Jeremiah, collector. O' Duilearga, Seamus, editor. 1944

A History of Ireland. Curtis, Edmund. 1936

The Story of Britain from the Romans to the Present. Fraser, Rebecca. 2006

Lovely is the Lee. Gibbings, Robert. 1945

The Corrib Country. Hayward, Richard. 1993

1,000 Years of Irish Poetry. Hoagland, Kathleen, editor. 1947

The Travellers: Ireland's Ethnic Minority. Burke, Mary, for the Imperial Archive "Project, Queen's University of Belfast." Litvack, Leon, supervisor. 2017

Annaghkeen. Love, Deborah. 1970

Ireland in Pre-Celtic Times. Macalister, Robert. 1921

In Search of Ancient Ireland. MacCaffrey, Carmel. 2002

The Middle Kingdom. MacManus, Dermot. 1959

Nine-Headed Dragon River. Matthiessen, Peter. 1986

The Snow Leopard. Matthiessen, Peter. 1978

Irish Travellers: Culture and Ethnicity. McCann, May, editor. 1994

A Concise History of Ireland. O'Brien, Maire and Conor Cruise. 1980

The Irish, A Character Study. O'Faolain, Sean. 1949

The Gestalt Approach and Eye Witness to Therapy. Perls, Fritz. 1989

The Irish Reader. Russell, Diarmuid. 1946

Report on Work in Sensory Awareness and Total Functioning. Selver, Charlotte. 1968

The Face and Mind of Ireland. Ussher, Arland. 1950

The Wisdom of Insecurity. Watts, Alan. 1951

The Way of Zen. Watts, Alan. 1957

Wilde's Lough Corrib. Wilde, Sir William. 1867

The Boyne and the Blackwater. Wilde, Sir William. 1849

Irish Folk Stories and Fairy Tales. Yeats, William Butler. 1888

About the Author

Rue Matthiessen is based on the East End of Long Island and in New York City. At Bard College she majored in literature, and afterwards was a journalist for *The East Hampton Star*. She had her own photography studio in Los Angeles for six years. Her essays and short fiction have been published in numerous literary journals. Her book, *Buttonwood Cottage*, about renovating a house in the Caribbean, is available on Amazon. She is currently at work on a novel, *Julia with Closed Eyes*. Recently, Rue was featured in the Bridgehampton Museum's Distinguished Lecture Series and other speaking engagements. See more at ruematthiessen.com